Practical Lessons In Leadership
A GUIDEBOOK FOR ASPIRING AND EXPERIENCED LEADERS

Art Petty and Rich Petro

Trafford
PUBLISHING

Note for Librarians: A cataloguing record for this book is available from Library and Archives Canada at www.collectionscanada.ca/amicus/index-e.html

Printed in Victoria, BC, Canada.

ISBN: 978-1-4251-2249-2

We at Trafford believe that it is the responsibility of us all, as both individuals and corporations, to make choices that are environmentally and socially sound. You, in turn, are supporting this responsible conduct each time you purchase a Trafford book, or make use of our publishing services. To find out how you are helping, please visit www.trafford.com/responsiblepublishing.html

Our mission is to efficiently provide the world's finest, most comprehensive book publishing service, enabling every author to experience success. To find out how to publish your book, your way, and have it available worldwide, visit us online at www.trafford.com/10510

 **Trafford** PUBLISHING™ www.trafford.com

North America & international
toll-free: 1 888 232 4444 (USA & Canada)
phone: 250 383 6864 ◆ fax: 250 383 6804 ◆ email: info@trafford.com

The United Kingdom & Europe
phone: +44 (0)1865 722 113 ◆ local rate: 0845 230 9601
facsimile: +44 (0)1865 722 868 ◆ email: info.uk@trafford.com

10 9 8 7 6 5 4 3

To Allison, Kyle & Michael
&
Mom, Dad & Adam
With my thanks and love.
-Art

To Mom, Dad, Sydney, Leigh, Libby and Ross-
You helped me understand that the opportunities
to be a leader are everywhere.
Thanks for your support.
-Rich

ACKNOWLEDGMENTS

Our sincere thanks to the many that inspired, motivated and challenged us to produce our best work. We owe our reviewers, Steve Wallin, Corrie Brague, Barb Bielawski and Bill Leonard a debt of gratitude for their time and insightful comments, corrections and suggestions. We owe Bill our additional thanks for his two round-trips through the manuscript and for providing us with the wisdom of his life and leadership experiences.

Thank you to the research sponsors and their teams along with the many individuals that participated in the process for your thoughtful feedback on what it means to lead. A special thanks to the sponsors and teams at Best Buy, Inc., Aon Consulting, Organic Valley Family of Farms, Inc. and the YMCA District of Lake County for their extraordinary help with this process.

Art owes a personal debt of gratitude to a group of people that provided the inspiration and motivation for his part of this work. Thanks to my early mentors: Don Cullen and Dennis Charlebois. And thank you to my 1L family: Leah Stussy, Stephanie Peterson, Trish Harman, Chris Colbert, Chris Lien, Julie Marks, Kristin Bjerke, Kristin McMahon, Jeanne Harshaw, Linda Droessler, Penny Gralewski, Sam Fellows, Amy Meyer, Joe Zurawski, Frank Dravis, Jack Kalander, Mike Keilen, Micki Heidtke, Steve Varsolona, Lou Peduto, Steve Shissler, Laura Riesterer-Randa, Brian King, Rick Juhl and Susan Becker. Thank you to Eric Lieberman and Paul Byrne for the opportunity to lead and to Rich Petro for joining me on this journey. All of you have left an indelible impression on me.

Rich is thankful for the HR team members he worked with, particularly Mark Hillard, Janet Viane, Kris Weber, Julie Dalton, DeeDee Stapleton-Hanc, Sharon Navarette, Delaina Doll Gardner, Sarah Lange, Jackie Ripp, Tracey Simpson and Karen Long. I learned more from you than you will ever know. Thanks as well to Eric and Paul – not just for the opportunity but also for the tolerance and support you both demonstrated. Finally, a special thanks to Art for providing the inspiration and invitation for this ride.

ABOUT THE AUTHORS

Art Petty is a successful leader, strategist, team-builder and trainer with over twenty years experience directing the growth, global expansion and rise to market leadership of large and small organizations in a variety of industries.

Art's employer and client list includes firms in the software, business intelligence, professional services, electronics, life safety, building automation, retail automation, direct marketing and mailing automation markets in the U.S., Europe and Asia. Professionally, he is unabashedly proud of the many successful teams he has created and the many people that have grown their careers under his leadership. Art lives with his wife and two sons in Crystal Lake, Illinois.

Rich Petro is an accomplished executive leader with nearly twenty-five years of human resources experience in settings varying from manufacturing to services to software, large and small organizations, and both private and public entities.

Rich blends a comprehensive understanding of all facets of human resources with solid business acumen to develop unique, forward-thinking solutions to the most challenging problems. Rich is an accomplished speaker and presenter, and has personally developed many programs and seminars on topics that included compliance, leadership philosophy and applied leadership skills. Rich is the father of two daughters and a son, and lives with his wife in Onalaska, Wisconsin.

CONTENTS

Introduction by the Authors xi
How to Use This Book xv

Part One: To Lead or Not to Lead?
A Crisis Catches Apex Off-Guard 3
1. The Motivation to Lead and the Nine
    Attributes of Great Leaders. 7
2. Solo Performer or Leader—A Guide to How the World Looks
    from Each Side of the Ladder 21
3. Leadership—How Do I Get There From Here? 39

Part Two: Succeeding from the Start. . . . .
4. The Top Ten Challenges that You Face as a (New) Leader 59
5. Congratulations, You Have a Team! Now What?. 73

Part Three: Succeeding All of the Time
6. Growing Your Personal Credibility Account 97
7. Forget Everything Else, Here's Your Real Job—Creating the
    Effective Work Environment. 115
8. The Power of Paying Attention to Your People 131
9. "No One Ever Told Me That Before."
    Leveraging Feedback as a Powerful Leadership Tool 145
10. Chief Talent Scout and Developer 167

Part Four: Tying It All Together to Drive Results
11. Creating a Culture of Innovation with Your Team 187
12. In Pursuit of Operational Excellence 203

Afterword: Looking Ahead in Your Career 215

INTRODUCTION BY THE AUTHORS

This is the book that I had to write to give back to aspiring leaders some of what I have learned during the past twenty-two years leading and managing teams. I am grateful that Rich took a look at the early content and agreed to apply his deep expertise in human resources and management and add some tremendous value in the process. His contributions strengthened the work considerably and added great enjoyment to the labor of writing. This is our book, and while we each may have been inspired to pursue the difficult task of writing for different reasons, we both share a common belief that leadership is a noble calling and that the development of leaders is an essential but often overlooked task in too many organizations.

For the aspiring professional, the choice to lead or not to lead is often made without the benefit of understanding the real work that will need to be done, or whether they have the skills, patience and fortitude to develop into an effective or even great leader. There are many great books on leadership, management, execution and strategy, but there are very few books that tie the pieces together into a digestible and actionable format for the new leader. While writing a "How To" book on becoming a great leader may seem challenging or even ridiculous, there are many insights, approaches and practices that when understood and applied, will improve the performance of the leader as well as the productivity and effectiveness of the entire team. These practices and approaches are borne from many years of trial and error, success and failure and endless exposure to market and business challenges.

We in business create a cycle where we take our most talented people and provide them career growth through leadership opportunities, ignoring the reality that there is nothing more difficult in the world than leading other human beings. It is this cycle that this book aspires to break, by providing the insight on what it means to lead, the guidance on becoming a leader and the approaches to executing the leadership task in the best interests and with the best results for the organization, the team and the individual as leader.

The inscription on the Alma Mater statue at the University of Illinois in Urbana-Champaign, reads, "To thy happy children of the future, those of the past send our greetings." It is in this spirit that I send my earnest greetings to the great leaders of the future in the hope that something in this book will contribute to your education, your development and your success.

> *-Arthur E. Petty at Crystal Lake, Illinois on this first day of March, 2007.*

Art had a vision for this book that hooked me from the start. His enthusiasm and passion for this topic is nothing short of infectious, and after working together for more than 6 years as part of the same executive team we plowed a great deal of ground together on people and leadership issues. There was absolutely no question in my mind that we had practical and valuable information to share as a result of this time together, in addition to our discreet past experiences. If you have been to the business section of the bookstore you know there are tons of books on leadership concepts and case studies. The selection is pretty paltry, however, at the applied end of the shelf. I was confident we could meaningfully add to it.

There is a cathartic aspect to writing on a topic about which you have experience and that you have a love for, but I wasn't in this for the therapy. If not for me, then, who is this work for? I have a few ideas:

- I can see far-reaching impact from this book. The world's need for more and better leaders is not limited to the commercial enterprise. Service organizations, youth groups, schools, churches, sports teams and yes, even the political realm stands to benefit if we all do a better job of preparing, selecting and developing candidates for leadership. Granted, the leadership role in many of those settings is a function of somebody being willing or gullible enough to volunteer (when is the last time you can remember having too many candidates to coach the youth soccer team?) but why limit our thinking. If my collaboration with Art has taught me anything, it's to aim high and don't settle for OK. Every time there are two or more people working on a common cause, for whatever the reason, they deserve a great leader.

INTRODUCTION

- I believe small and medium sized organizations have the most to gain from this book. They usually don't have the infrastructure, institutionalized practices or economies of scale that are the foundations of world-class leadership development efforts in large firms, but they still need to develop leaders. If those organizations can get this book into the hands of new and aspiring leaders they will be off to a great start.

- The development process starts with who gets into the leadership community in the first place. In nearly 25 years of human resources experience I have come face to face with far too many Peter-Principled leaders: well-intentioned career moves where the subject is promoted into a role for which they are ill-suited. The result was usually dramatic – or should I say problematic – for the individuals they tried to lead and the organizations they were expected to serve. These misplaced leaders not only under-perform in delivering results, they are equally deficient at developing the people entrusted to their care. I firmly believe our work can blot up quite a bit of the spilled organizational milk of poor leadership selection, and make many people happier in the process.

- For all of these reasons it is my hope that sharing what we learned proves to be a benefit to many people and organizations. Use it, pass it on and recommend it. Like all great written works – and even average ones – it does no good sitting on the shelf gathering dust.

-Rich Petro at Onalaska, Wisconsin on this first day of March, 2007

HOW TO USE THIS BOOK

It's impossible to substitute experience with a book, but every leg of every journey can benefit from a roadmap at times. Whether you are thinking about leadership as a career choice, or you have ten or twenty years of experience leading teams, we are willing to bet our reputations that there is something of value for you between these covers.

For the aspiring or early career leader, a few hours invested in cover-to-cover reading will provide clear context for your role, warn you of common new leader pitfalls and offer suggestions to help drive results for your firm. The beauty of this book is that we not only create awareness of <u>what</u> the challenges are, we give you guidance on <u>how</u> to flourish when you encounter them.

The experienced leader will profit from their time with this book as well. The many practical and powerful suggestions for increasing your credibility, improving your team's work environment and motivating and driving innovation and operational excellence will help you improve results and remember why you loved leading in the first place. And importantly, as an experienced leader with the priority to develop new leaders, this book should serve as a guide for you. It is a ready reference on topics ranging from helping to identify individuals with leadership talent to ensuring that you are providing the right level of coaching and support as they start-up in this challenging new role.

A few additional suggestions for optimizing your experience with the book:

- Part 1, "To Lead or Not to Lead?" offers essential advice and tools for anyone considering a role in leadership or anyone responsible for identifying new leaders.

- The Apex Integrated Technologies (a fictional company) case study that prefaces each chapter and the questions that follow the chapter are intended as discussion tools for group settings or projects. Each mini-case incorporates concepts included in the associated chapter and references issues commonly faced in a leadership setting. You can use the case contents and the questions in management roundtable settings or as a self-learning tool. Our thoughts on each vignette can be found at www.management-innovations.com in the leadership resource center, and we hope they add context to your discussions.

- The Resource Center at www.management-innovations.com includes added content, research papers, case studies, blogs, ideas and tools as well as links to our training courses and other offerings. Content relevant to the book can be unlocked by typing in the password: LEADER when prompted or by e-mailing us at knowledge@management-innovations.com

The book can be read cover to cover or in sections relevant to your current situation. We encourage you to highlight liberally, bend the pages where you find useful information and e-mail us at knowledge@management-innovations.com with questions or comments on the content and concepts. And most of all, we hope that you enjoy the journey and build enough experience to fill your own book!

PART ONE
TO LEAD OR NOT TO LEAD?

A CRISIS CATCHES APEX OFF-GUARD

---

*T*he leadership conference in January at Apex Integrated Technologies, Inc., was different this year. This annual gathering of all supervisors, managers, directors and executives was famous for its balanced mix of fun, socializing and business. This year, however, all thoughts that this meeting would be like past events evaporated during the CEO's keynote.

Victoria Pyott, Apex's CEO, kicked the meeting off with a series of warning messages that took everyone by surprise. Ms. Pyott expressed her opinion that changing market and competitor conditions were undermining Apex's position as a leader. She also raised concerns about the leadership team's focus on the right issues, including market monitoring, strategy evaluation and operational effectiveness. And those weren't her only concerns.

Victoria suggested that the leadership group had become complacent and had lost track of the two attributes of the culture that made the company the market leader and the employer of choice in this industry: innovation and the development of talent. These concerns struck a nerve in the group, and reluctantly they had to agree that the evidence supported Victoria's claims.

Customer satisfaction was down versus prior years, the revenue from new products had declined for the third straight year, involuntary turnover was up, open positions had climbed considerably, and employee satisfaction was down. The major news in the market was coming from competitive announcements, not Apex introductions, and internally, costs were heading in the wrong direction. Victoria's observation that the company was beginning to become siloed and that an inordinate amount of energy went into resolving turf wars and creating bureaucracy versus focusing on clients and partners, was icing on this sour cake.

Ms. Pyott closed her remarks with a call to action: "We will not succeed on our mission here at Apex if we lose track of who we are working for—our customers—and what we need to do to excite and delight them with our performance every step of the way. We also cannot sustain our hard-earned market *position or even expect to succeed in the future if we do not remember that the development of our employee talent and our future leaders are fundamental responsibilities of all managers. We need to spur a revolution in our business—rapid innovation in new products and services, significant improvement in our operating processes and a renewed commitment to building value for our stakeholders every single day."*

PREFACE TO CHAPTER 1

DWAYNE'S BAD DAY

Dwayne Edwards sat in his chair staring at the wall for a few minutes after Barb Kushing had left his office. Barb's resignation letter was on Dwayne's desk, and frankly, he was so upset about the situation, that he couldn't bear to look at it. He opened his top drawer, dropped in the letter and jammed it shut.

Dwayne was Vice President of Business Development at Apex Technologies, Inc., and had been working hard for three years to build a strong team. Barb was his right hand and heir apparent, and he was shocked at this new turn of events. She was leaving to join a competitor who had offered her a hefty raise to step into a role just like Dwayne's.

Along with the raise, Barb was being sponsored for an intensive general management development program at a major university, and she said she just couldn't pass up the entire package. She admitted she liked Dwayne and the work at Apex, but she felt like there was no plan for her or anyone's future, and didn't want to spin her wheels anymore. She indicated that she would prefer to stay with Apex, but without any support to her career aspirations, it just didn't make sense.

As he sat there, Dwayne recalled the other three resignations he had received over the last 18 months. "Good people, the future of our team and now they're gone," he thought with a sigh. It was true that Apex didn't have a formal career development program for employees, but he did everything he could to be a great boss and a friend to his team members. With the loss of key staff, it was getting harder to hit his targets, and with Barb walking out the door, he imagined his year-end bonus walking out with her.

CHAPTER 1
THE MOTIVATION TO LEAD AND THE
NINE ATTRIBUTES OF GREAT LEADERS

Most people don't pick up books on leadership for beach reading, and we suspect that you are no different. Either your boss suggested that this would be good for you, or you are an ambitious professional looking for an edge. Regardless of why you decided to crack the cover, we are glad you're here. If leadership is an important topic for you, either because that's where you want to be; or, you are already there and you want to get better at it, then this is the right place for you. Rich and I have attempted to jam our almost forty-five years of combined leadership experience into these pages, with the intent of providing you some practical ideas to help you along your career journey.

During the course of the book, you can expect a healthy blend of one part philosophy, two parts strategy and four parts how to be great at leading. From time to time, we'll add a dash of how we've seen people really stink at leading to counter-balance our over the top positive view on the noble profession of leadership. At all times however, we have your best interests at heart as we do our best to help you develop insights to successfully navigate the stormy seas of life as a leader.

In structuring this book the way we have, it is our intent to meet the needs of two groups: aspiring and experienced leaders. Aspiring leaders are the tougher audience to address, because they generally see moving into management as the best or only means to enhance their career, and this blinds them to understanding what they are getting themselves into. Chapters 1-3 are specifically written for this part of our audience, and will help these professionals develop a better understanding of the career issues and opportunities for a leader versus an individual contributor. The balance of the book is for everyone interested in doing a great job leading, whether you are brand new to the role, highly experienced, or just interested in what it takes to succeed in this profession. Following the career content in the first three chapters, the flow of the book takes a leader from starting up with a new team all the way through creating a culture of innovation and realizing an operationally excellent team. The content in-between offers timeless advice for building your credibility as a leader, becoming a great talent scout, and growing comfortable conducting the tough discussions that are important to all leaders.

Experienced leaders, or grizzled veterans as we describe them, offer one additional challenge for us in creating a book on leadership. It is our hope that they will see the content in this book as helpful to their mission to develop the next generation of leadership talent for their organizations. If you are charged with identifying and assisting in the development of new leaders, you can use this book as a tool to help your team members evaluate career options in leadership, get started after a promotion, and realize success by developing good habits early in their careers. We hope that you are the kind of boss that will take the time to leverage the philosophy, the pragmatic suggestions and the best practices that are resident between the cover pages of this book. The development of the next generation of leadership is an important undertaking, and it is our intent to provide you with some valuable assistance along the way.

A Little Housekeeping—Our Perspectives on Leadership

Before we embark on our leadership journey and dazzle you with compelling approaches to improve your effectiveness as a leader and drive great results for your firm, it is only fair that we provide you with an understanding of how we view the field of leadership. If you understand our basic philosophy about leaders and leading, then you will have context for the lessons and approaches outlined throughout the book. Besides, it is always good to understand what makes people tick when you are thinking about working together. Since we hope to be with you for a few hours now, and perhaps on a periodic basis throughout your career, here's the short-form about what makes us tick when it comes to the profession of leadership.

A Philosophy of Leading in Ten Easy Steps

1. Not everyone should lead.
2. No one should lead without understanding the role of a leader and doing some serious soul searching about the commitment required for success.
3. Leaders are mostly made...not born. (See #4)
4. Leading effectively is hard work. (See #3)
5. Great leaders have an underlying philosophy about leading— they operate with a charter.
6. Credibility is the leader's currency and effective leaders work unceasingly to strengthen theirs.
7. Effective leaders maintain a clear view of the external forces affecting their business and integrate all of their actions with an organization's strategy and key objectives.
8. Effective leaders understand that innovation and operational excellence are outcomes of an effective working environment.
9. Effective leaders are always on the lookout for talent, and are passionate about supporting the development of the next generation of leaders.
10. The best leaders never quit learning how to improve their skills.

You can begin to see a theme developing. We truly believe that leadership is a profession, and that like any profession, achieving competence or excellence requires hard work, dedication and the belief that what you are doing is important to others.

The New Leader Development Dilemma and the Evolving Leader Shortage

At least part of the motivation for us to write this book comes from our concern over the lack of formal leadership development practices in many organizations. Often highly qualified individual contributors (soloists) are tapped on the shoulder and asked to lead a team, without much more than a hearty thanks and a "go get 'em tiger," pat on the back from their well- intended, but naive managers. And, while some people are successful at navigating through the learning curve of a new leader, many individuals are frustrated with the unexpected challenges of motivating and guiding other human beings. The cost to an organization of this ad hoc leadership identification and development process can be significant. Of course, this dilemma is entirely preventable with the adoption of some common-sense leadership development practices that we happily outline in this book.

Add in an impending global shortage of leadership resources to the poor practices described above, and you understand another motivation for writing this book. The very visible and predicted demographic changes over the upcoming decade will result in a major change in the way organizations value and develop their leadership talent. Through 2014, the retirement of the baby boomer generation will create 76 million vacancies in the U.S. alone. From the writing of this book in 2006 through late 2010, it is estimated that half of the top leadership talent of the Fortune 500 will retire. With experienced leaders exiting the job market at an unprecedented pace, organizations will be stressed to find, train and retain the leadership talent necessary to run their businesses. Younger, less experienced workers will be challenged to assume leadership responsibility earlier in their careers and organizations will do everything possible to accommodate the demands for flexibility of boomers that might be willing to help out part-time. The net of all of this will be a rise in the value of leadership talent, and significant investment from organizations in the development of their leadership assets. Organizations that become great at developing leadership talent will enjoy a meaningful competitive advantage in the marketplace.

The expected bull market in leadership talent will be a great opportunity for professionals that understand how to motivate, inspire and drive great results with a diverse and often distributed workforce. Leadership skills are highly transferable so the philosophies, practices and approaches outlined here will play in any organization, regardless of industry. The next decade will be a remarkable time to be in leadership, and it is our fondest hope to contribute to the proliferation of best practices and great leaders.

Leading Effectively is Hard Work and Not Everyone Should Lead

While not wanting to throw cold water on anyone's ambitions, both Rich and I feel duty-bound to get two key messages out on the table: leading effectively is hard work, and leadership is not for everyone. The best leaders work hard at their jobs, because they understand the impact that they can have on the morale, productivity and creativity of their team. They also understand that it is their job to create a working environment that produces operational excellence and stimulates a culture of innovation. They work hard on proving their credibility as leaders by treating people with respect, backing their words with actions and putting the interests of their team members ahead of their own. They also understand that to be successful, they need to pay attention to their people, offering help and development support when needed, and conducting the tough discussions when necessary. Effective leaders are often great teachers, ensuring that their team's activities are grounded in what is going on in the marketplace and focused on executing around an organization's strategies. These leaders don't punch a time-clock, and often are frustrated that they only have so much time in a day to help support their team's efforts. Most of all, effective leaders work and work, and then they work some more, not because it is their job, but because leading is their chosen profession. If you are allergic to hard work, you might want to consider another path for your career.

Not Everyone Should Lead

One of the frequent challenges of an experienced manager is dealing with and supporting the career aspirations of their team members. This is a good challenge with many rewards and a few frustrations as well. One of the more interesting dilemmas is dealing with aspiring professionals that indicate that they are ready for a management role. By using a few probing questions, the manager can quickly ascertain how well their ambitious associate has thought through this career step, and importantly, how well they understand what they might be getting themselves into as a new leader.

Seven Questions for the Ambitious Aspiring Leader

1. Why do you want to lead other people?
2. What do you think the true role of a leader is?
3. Do you understand that the skills that make you successful as an individual contributor are not the skills you need to succeed as a leader?
4. Are you prepared to give up domain expertise as your foundation for results?
5. What do you believe are the skills and personality traits that you need as a leader?

6. Do you understand that you will be responsible for the output of your team members, and that you will be judged on this output?

7. What do you imagine your workday life to be like as a leader?

Whether you are reading these questions through the eyes of the ambitious aspiring leader or the grizzled veteran that we referenced earlier, these questions are critical to both of you. As the aspiring leader, you need to understand that moving into a management role is not a continuation of your current job, but rather a fundamental shift in your career. You owe it to yourself, to your boss and to your organization to carefully think through and answer these questions as honestly as possible. If you don't have a passion for helping people and the fortitude to execute on the key challenges that a leader faces, then you should remain as a valued individual contributor. As for the grizzled veteran, you are charged with coaching and developing leadership talent and for strengthening your organization in every possible way. You owe it to all parties to help your team members make informed career decisions, and to ensure that people are not put into situations where they lack the understanding and skills necessary to succeed. In Chapter 2, Rich offers up a treasure trove of tools to help both of you work through the issue of "to lead or not to lead?"

Effective Leaders Understand and Adhere to The True Role of A Leader

Whether you are focusing on developing your own skills as a leader, or you are helping someone understand what it means to lead; I believe that it is important to be able to describe the role in overarching terms. Early in my career, I crafted a description of the role of a leader to help remind me of my priorities and taped it to my office wall. As I assumed responsibility for developing new leaders later in my career, I found this now dog-eared piece of paper with the run-on sentence to be remarkably helpful in counseling aspiring and new leaders on the nature of their real job. This *Leader's Charter* is a powerful description of the nature and scope of a leader's true role.

The Leader's Charter

> *Your primary role as a leader is to <u>create an environment</u> that facilitates high individual and team performance against company and industry standards, supports innovation in processes, programs and approaches, encourages*

collaboration where necessary for objective achievement and promotes the development of your associates in roles that leverage their talents and interests and that challenge them to new and greater accomplishments.

There are many important concepts linked together in the charter, and while we will explore them in detail during the course of the book, this is important context to help you understand our philosophy of leading and for you to begin creating a visual of yourself as a leader. As I've used this tool over time, I've encouraged people to challenge it, add to or suggest deleting components, but as of yet, no one has disagreed with the philosophy or the contents. Very few job descriptions will adequately define this role, so consider this your real job description.

Leadership as a Profession and The Nine Attributes of Great Leaders

One of our manuscript reviewers offered the perspective that "leadership is a profession with a body of knowledge waiting to be discovered." He said it with a chuckle, and was quick to qualify that he didn't know if he made that up or heard it during the course of his career as a management trainer. Regardless of the origin, his observation was truly insightful. Experience is the best teacher for leadership, with the most important lessons learned by doing and often by failing. While we cannot fast forward through time so that you gain critical experience, we can arm you with our ideas about what makes a great leader, and suggestions to move you along that path. Like *The Leader's Charter* that provides context for the role of a leader, *The Nine Attributes of Great Leaders* describes the attributes and habits of leaders that make a positive difference in the world and in our lives. We refer to *The Nine Attributes* frequently throughout the book, and we encourage you to add to our list as you form your own perspective on what makes a great leader.

The Nine Attributes of Great Leaders

1. Great leaders realize that their role is less about themselves and more about what they can do to encourage and aid the development of the people around them.

    As a leader, you are never the subject or focal point of your team's activities. It takes a great deal of maturity and emotional intelligence to recognize that you exist to support and develop the team, and that victories are to the team's credit while defeats are your responsibility. As a leader, all of your energy must be focused on helping others succeed through aligning their talents with key challenges and then providing the tools and support that your team members need to succeed.

If you enjoy being in the spotlight, gaining credit and accolades for your accomplishments, or you prefer to focus solely on what you can do to solve a problem, it is likely that you are better suited for the role of individual contributor. Great leaders stand in the shadows and ensure that the spotlight shines directly on their team members. The satisfaction of knowing that they created the environment for their team members to succeed is reward enough.

2. Great leaders are driven to positively affect their business and their people. They expect the near impossible from themselves and their charges and they live by the code of accountability.

The most effective leaders are driven by the need to achieve. They understand that the organization has entrusted valuable human resources to them, and they understand that in return for this trust, the organization is entitled to a high level of achievement around strategic objectives. Their drive to succeed is innate, and their confidence, enthusiasm and passion for the game of business are visible and infectious to all. Additionally, great leaders practice their profession with a strict code of accountability, where they, along with everyone on their team, are responsible for achievement of necessary targets. The combination of drive, focus on objectives and accountability contribute to the creation of the effective working environment that is so critical to success.

3. Great leaders realize that they are human and make mistakes. They also understand that it is ok for everyone to see and learn from their mistakes.

Great leaders are self-confident enough to allow their own mistakes to be visible, and to leverage those mistakes for learning opportunities. Their self-confidence to showcase their own mistakes contributes to creating a culture of risk-taking and innovation that are essential to the team's success.

4. Great leaders understand that they are being constantly scrutinized to see if their actions match their words.

   The most effective leaders are aware that they are under constant scrutiny from their team members as well as their peers and managers. They wear their intentions on their shirtsleeves and they avoid gamesmanship like the plague. They also understand that their words leave deep imprints on people, and that if their actions diverge from their words, they are damaging their own credibility.

5. Great leaders are driven by a love of teaching and a passion for learning.

   Great leaders are great teachers and great students, both by example and by practice. The daily job of a leader is to teach others how to succeed, how to innovate or how to overcome problems. The most powerful teaching comes from helping people learn how to understand the nature of problems and providing guidance on approaches to constructing solutions, without providing the solution. In addition, these dedicated teachers are equally dedicated to learning and to seeking out new opportunities and experiences that will challenge them and add to their body of knowledge, which in-turn is incorporated into their teachings.

6. Great leaders understand the impact that they have on the people around them and they keep this in mind when praising and criticizing.

   Hallway executions and public criticism destroy credibility and the working environment. Great leaders understand that even the most casual of conversations are impactful to their charges and they take great care to talk clearly, measure their words and learn how to deliver criticism constructively and privately. Alternatively, the most effective leaders leverage praise as a powerful, constructive tool, providing it judiciously but visibly where earned, and resisting the urge to use it as a false motivational tool. Too much praise or praise for trivial matters dilutes its effectiveness and too little praise is destructive to the working environment.

7. Great leaders make a lot of decisions because they understand the power that they wield to either slowdown or accelerate progress through their decision-making.

Decision-making determines pace, and the leader that makes more decisions is more effective than the leader that will not make a decision. The style of the leader in this area is a powerful component of the working environment, and is visible and tangible to the entire team.

The leader that is slow to make a decision is often driven by politics and the concern that if the decision is wrong it will fall on his shoulders. This leader frustrates his associates by slowing or reducing their productivity and ultimately, destroying morale. Alternatively, the effective leader understands that their role is to make decisions quickly (albeit with the best available information to guide the decision), and that every decision is a building block in pursuit of achievement. The faster the decisions, the faster the progress occurs, even with the possibility of the occasional misfire.

The decision-making leader knows he is accountable, but understands that the individual and team performances are more important to his success than the occasional wrong choice is to his potential failure.

8. Great leaders understand that their primary role is to create the proper working environment necessary for success given the circumstances and talent at the time.

The leader is critically aware of the impact that the working environment has on her team. She understands that her personal credibility is at the heart of building the effective working environment, and she focuses on building the positive personal credibility necessary for people to place their trust in her leadership.

Outstanding leaders understand that accomplishment is driven by individuals and teams willing and comfortable taking risks and pursuing innovation. They strive to ensure that the working environment motivates and rewards those behaviors at all times. They also understand that the right working environment varies with talent and circumstances, and they manage this variable to meet those changing conditions.

9. Great leaders know that they need quality people to succeed and they constantly focus on the identification and development of these individuals.

    The most successful leaders are those that understand that they need to match tasks with talent and vice-versa, and that it is their full-time job to seek out, secure and develop this talent. They understand that there are different roles that people play…talented soloists or great collaborators, and they ensure that the structure is built to execute the strategy and that the talent is properly aligned within the structure.

Epilogue

Establishing yourself as a great leader, or even an effective leader, requires a remarkable amount of self-awareness, self-confidence, humility, ego and hard work. While self-confidence and ego might seemingly conflict with humility, it is a balancing act that only the most mature can manage. You need the self-confidence and ego to develop and motivate people to great achievements and you need the humility to understand that YOU are not the subject of your team's endeavors. As you consider moving down the path of leadership in your career, take the time to examine your true motivations by answering the *Seven Questions for the Ambitious Aspiring Leader,* and gain insight for the role and attributes of a leader through *The Leader's Charter* and *The Nine Attributes of Great Leaders.* If you are an experienced leader seeking to develop you leadership talent pool, leverage those same tools in discussion with your team members.

Regardless of whether you are experienced, aspiring or newly minted leader, you should remember to continually invest in yourself and your development as a leader. You've chosen a difficult profession where your actions and approaches will have lasting impact on the people you lead. You owe it to yourself, your company and your team members to aspire to be great in this capacity. Some suggestions for developing your leadership education include:

- Read this book cover to cover and leverage the tools and approaches suggested throughout. Save it and re-read it from time to time, especially the chapters on building your credibility, creating the effective working environment, handling the tough conversations and creating innovative and operationally excellent teams. If you are responsible for developing new leaders, the first three chapters should become a part of your toolkit, and should be required reading for aspiring leaders.

- As you identify leaders in your own environment that fit the archetype of the great leader, seek these people out and learn from them. If your firm has a formal mentoring program, take advantage of it, and if not, create your own.
- Read voraciously, occasionally from business books, but mostly from history and biographies of people that were challenged with seemingly insurmountable obstacles and overcame those obstacles.
- As you progress in your career, take advantage of executive education opportunities in leadership. These can be powerful, and if your company will pay the bill, you would be insane not to take advantage of this opportunity.
- Visit the Resources Center at www.management-innovations.com for inspirational and helpful content, including suggested readings, case studies in leadership and practical suggestions for improving your effectiveness as a leader and driving great results for your organization.

And finally, don't forget to ask the people you interact with on a daily basis about what you can do better. If you have established effective working relationships and focused on building your personal credibility, you may be surprised at the quality and honesty of the constructive feedback that you receive. Remember, leadership like life is a journey and the fun occurs along the way, not at the destination.

Discussion questions-Dwayne's Bad Day

- *What can Dwayne do to stop losing good people?*
- *Is the problem Dwayne's or Apex's?*
- *Should Dwayne counter Barb's offer in an attempt to get her to stay?*
- *Based on Victoria's comments in the opening preface and Dwayne's problem with losing talent, what steps would you recommend that Apex take to improve the situation?*
- *Can individual leaders compensate for the lack of formal or corporate-wide talent development programs?*

For ideas on how the authors view the situation at Apex and the issues outlined above, visit the Leadership Resource Center at www.management-innovations. com, and click on Practical Lessons-Discussion Questions.

PREFACE TO CHAPTER 2

PAT'S DILEMMA

Pat Paulsen nudged her car forward in the line of traffic merging on to the interstate on a gray, chilly morning. The unusually slow ride to work gave her time to think about how she would manage her day's agenda at Apex Inc. She was worried about two meetings in particular, both performance reviews. She would be conducting reviews with Bob Hobson and Susan Smith, and both had made it clear that they were interested in the open supervisor's position in the Customer Support Department. Neither had managed before, but both had a strong case to make for their contributions to the department.

Pat had to admit that she wasn't sure what to do. Bob was her technical star, coming to the rescue of every tough technical problem, and tremendously respected for this knowledge by the customers and internal staff that he helped. On the other hand, Susan seemed to be a natural leader. Her technical skills were not as strong as Bob's, but for the last year, Susan had proven herself capable of pulling together groups to solve problems or lead projects, and she clearly was well-liked by her peers. The choice was tough. Two good people, both very different, and she didn't want to lose either one of them if she could avoid it.

Pat knew that she needed to make the right decision. With the call to action issued by their CEO, Victoria Pyott, Pat knew that strengthening the leadership culture at Apex was a top priority. Additionally, customer satisfaction numbers were heading in the wrong direction, and it would be important for the new supervisor to be a strong contributor to solving this problem. If only she had two promotions to offer, she wouldn't be in this dilemma.

The Candidates

Susan arrived early that morning to spend a few minutes organizing her thoughts. She really wanted the supervisor role, but she was concerned that her average technical skills were going to hurt her during the interview. Her plan was to emphasize her strong interpersonal skills and to showcase a number of the group projects that she spearheaded during the year. She knew she was up against Bob, and that she would need every edge that she could get.

Bob strolled through the door at the crack of 8:15 a.m., his usual time fifteen minutes after the company start. He smiled to himself thinking about today's review with Pat and about his chances for the promotion. Bob knew that his that his skills were legendary around Apex, and he planned to play them up for everything that they were worth.

CHAPTER 2
SOLO PERFORMER OR LEADER—A GUIDE TO HOW THE WORLD LOOKS FROM EACH SIDE OF THE LADDER

Deciding what to be when you grow up is one of life's biggest challenges. When you think about your own childhood aspirations, you might remember an early desire to be a fireman or a dancer. That likely morphed into a somewhat more thoughtful interest in being a professional athlete or an actor. As your understanding of the world matured, and you had an expectation that you would go to college, you almost certainly thought about becoming a doctor or lawyer. So how did you end up as a marketing communication specialist, cost accountant or a benefits analyst? You can be assured most professionals have traveled a circuitous path to reach their present role. Interest, effort, job availability, market conditions, expense, reality, the influence of friends and family all played a part in determining that path. Those same influencers will play a part in the path your career takes going forward, but the guidance in this chapter will help assure your are the primary architect of your career.

The career planning process is typically not well understood by the leaders who are entrusted with the development of aspiring professionals. More often than not career moves are reactionary. They are not made with the benefit of careful, insightful guidance, much less formal planning. Organizations may have invested in potential outcomes of career planning but not in the process. Firms dedicate time and energy to performance review, feedback and goal setting training with the assumption that the product of these initiatives will be growing, successful professionals. The reality is often different.

From the perspective of the aspiring professional contemplating a leadership role as the next step in your career, let's characterize your decision-making as a dichotomy: to lead or not to lead. In this chapter we provide insight into the characteristics of individual contributor roles and how they compare to leadership roles. We'll examine everything from social perceptions to compensation to skills for each side of the career ladder. Our objective is not to unduly influence you one way or the other, but to provide you the means and confidence to make a decision about whether a career in leadership is right for you.

Leader or Individual Contributor—Key Characteristics of Each Role

So what is it like to be a leader on a day-to-day basis and how does it compare to life as an individual contributor? How will you spend your time as a leader? How will people view you now that you are a supervisor? Alternatively, what are the potential benefits of staying as a soloist? How will you be able to contribute to your organization's success in this capacity? What are some of the advantages of staying independent? These are all important questions that must be answered when considering the move to a leadership role. Granted, you have seen leadership positions executed by others, but it is not always apparent what goes on behind the scenes. The following summary will compare and contrast many of the characteristics of these two roles.

WORKING LIFESTYLE

Individual Contributor

Infrequent demands on your time beyond 9-5 except with certain roles. Work-related issues are more likely left at work. Stress is often centered on tangible things such as deliverables, deadlines and sometimes problem-solving.

Leader

The higher the level, the less likely the work is to revolve around the clock or calendar. Plan to have constant 'contact capability' with your peers, manager and perhaps customers. Expect to take work home, to ball games, on vacation, etc. Stress often comes from less tangible, 'what if' aspects of this role.

REGARD FROM OTHERS

Individual Contributor

Centers around the kind of work you do, and your tenure with a given organization or industry. Consideration is given for individual achievements. Esteem is more often earned through subject matter expertise, and reputation for results than tenure.

Leader

Results more from your role/title and less about you as an individual. Esteem is earned by those who are successful in developing, promoting and finding opportunities for capable people. Title is often less indicative of the work you actually do, and is best understood by other like-placed professionals.

PERSONAL RELATIONSHIPS AT WORK

Individual Contributor

Probably have a close friend within your functional area with whom to commiserate over work and personal issues. This relationship not likely to be affected by changes in grade as an individual contributor, but may change if one party is promoted to a leadership role.

Leader

A close friend is more likely to be developed within your 'level' versus functional area. This relationship is likely to change if one party moves more than one level away from the other. You are likely to have to make a business decision that touches an existing personal relationship at some point in your career.

RELATIONSHIPS WITH OTHERS IN THE ORGANIZATION

Individual Contributor

Complementary relationships with peers are the norm. Your contributions add value to the work of other individuals or teams and vice versa. Generally need to be comfortable with people who are likely to be similar to you.

Leader

Complex networks exemplify these roles. Staying informed and delivering results for the organization as a whole necessitates a web of interactions across levels and functional areas. Need to be comfortable with diverse people and with all levels of the organization.

TIME ORIENTATION

Individual Contributor

Tend to focus on present, near term deliverables.

Leader

Some near term focus, but largely focused on future deliverables, capability.

TASK ORIENTATION

Individual Contributor

Characterized by task work, projects, and problems to work on. Delivery dates/deadlines and quality of work expectations typically determined by others, but may be less so in specialized, high level roles.

Leader

Less individual task work, decreasing as you move up. More time spent in oversight of others' deliverables, relationship building, and planning.

ACCOUNTABILITY

Individual Contributor

Accountable for your own work, and to a lesser degree, collaborating with others. You will be largely responsible for assuring your own skills stay applicable, competitive.

Leader

Emphasis on deliverables executed by others. Additional emphasis on collaboration within your team and across teams. You are judged primarily by how much you get out of others, but characteristics beyond pure output are also critical. Establishing an environment that is creative and collaborative is important. Developing others will also be a key requirement.

ORGANIZATIONAL IMPACT

Individual Contributor

May be narrow but deep. Focus will be on specific product, technology, capability, etc. Subject matter or process expertise brings value. Opportunity for thought leadership within and beyond the organization.

Leader

Broad influence beyond the individual or team. Process and outcome-oriented. More likely to have influence in strategic, direction-setting matters. Less focus on domain expertise, which decreases as you move up. Your value is more a function of what you can deliver and the impact you have on results as opposed to what you know.

JOB RISK

Individual Contributor

Less risk of losing your position in lean times. Individual exposure is minimal, less likely to create circumstances where a problem or error would result in termination.

Leader

Greater risk of position elimination in difficult times. Management is first and foremost considered overhead – an expense that can be reduced or eliminated in return for preserving a position of those 'doing the work'. On the other hand, effective leaders can be successful in different settings or industries but making the switch may be difficult. There are significantly fewer leadership roles in every organization than individual contributors – typically outnumbered by factor of at least 10 to 1.

COMPENSATION

Individual Contributor

Total Planned Compensation (TPC) will be largely comprised of base pay. If you are eligible for variable pay (bonus, incentive pay) it will be a very small portion of your TPC. Minimal volatility in annual earnings. Variable pay may be based on factors that are closer to your own control or shared with others. Earning potential will be less than the higher levels of leadership roles, but high-level individual contributor positions will be comparable to the first couple levels of leadership positions.

Leader

Total Planned Compensation (TPC) will have a larger component of variable pay than individual contributors. As such, it is often considered at-risk pay. As a result, variations in year over year earnings can be dramatic. Variable pay is more likely to be factored on 'greater good' components such as overall organizational results and to a lesser degree your team's specific results.

What should you get out of these summaries? We hope they paint a picture of a leader's selflessness in pursuit of organizational goals while putting personal needs on the back burner. Leadership roles are never about YOU and if you approach them that way you are destined to fail. Probably not just fail, but go down in a large ball of flame with a cheering crowd of gas can holders all around you. OK, maybe that is a little hyperbolic but the message you should take away is that leaders are only effective if they can get things done with and through others, for the greater common good. That has to be a fundamental belief for you to be a success. In addition, some self-sacrifice will be expected as these roles are not completed in a 9-5 format and don't stay in the desk or computer at the end of the traditional workweek.

The Compensation Issue

You probably noticed that compensation was the last characteristic summarized. It wasn't an accident. We will keep drumming this one point into you: if you are doing it solely for the money you are missing the point of being a leader. If you are not excited about contributing to an organization's success through the coordinated actions of others, if you don't get pumped by seeing others take on challenges they didn't believe they could tackle, and if you are not absolutely committed to making decisions for the greater good above individual recognition, please step aside. If you can do all these things successfully you deserve the money, but if the money is the primary motivation for pursuing a leadership role, again, please step aside.

In fairness, compensation is an important factor in everybody's life. You should be vigilant in understanding and planning your financial future, but when you are thinking about your life's work it should not start with money. Some people are truly motivated by money and that is not a bad thing. My experience has put these people in two camps – the highly competitive who see earnings as a way to keep score, and the people who define success by the materialistic "Rolex method" who are willing to do whatever they have to do to get it. My experience has also shown that the former is more likely to be successful, and the latter may make a bunch of money for a period of time but won't sustain a highly-paid role, and their career will be characterized by hopping from organization to organization with increasingly shorter stints and increasingly longer periods between opportunities before a significant lifestyle change is required. These are certainly not the hallmarks of thoughtful career planning.

Leader or Individual Contributor—Skills Comparison

Now that you have a summary of what's it like to be in a leadership role let's move on to what it takes. The following is a table of skill differences between individual contributor and leadership roles. These tables reflect a very broad, high-level comparison of the attributes that are indicators of potential success in these two kinds of roles. There are many common success factors between the roles, so we will concentrate on a few key areas of difference.

COMMUNICATION SKILLS

Individual Contributor

Ability to report status, describe problems, need for assistance. Break down complex technical or domain-specific issues into easily understood parcels.

Leader

Ability to influence, motivate others. Capable of conveying vision and expected outcomes while encouraging the pursuit of results that exceed the norm.

COLLABORATION

Individual Contributor

Individual contributor roles almost always require one to play well with others. The ability to work interdependently with peers – including those in different functional areas – can be vital to complete your personal tasks.

Leader

Set an example by maintaining productive relationships throughout the organization, and at all levels. Responsible for building an environment that encourages groups of varied individuals to work well together in order to produce their best work.

TIME MANAGEMENT

Individual Contributor

Ability to use time wisely on a daily, weekly basis. A tactical focus. Ability to manage occasional longer-term projects within guidelines set by others.

Leader

Balance capacity, throughput and long-term deliverables for a group of others, typically in light of shifting priorities. A strategic focus with longer time horizons and broader implications. Ability to adjust the priorities of others prior to calamity as conditions warrant.

TASK ORIENTATION

Individual Contributor

Get things done on time with high quality results such as meeting or exceeding requirements and expectations, limited need for re-do's, etc.

Leader

Empowerment and delegation are key – assign day-to-day work and get out of the way. Ability to resist doing the work yourself.

DELEGATION

Individual Contributor

Work assignments determined by others. May give assignments in a more senior role, but otherwise delegation is limited to managing 'hand-offs' of work from those who may be upstream or downstream of your process

Leader

Ability to make direct requests for assignments to be carried out by others. Can include undesirable tasks, with onerous expectations for challenge, time constraints, etc. As a first-level manager expect to give direction to associates who may be older and longer tenured.

DEVELOPING OTHERS

Individual Contributor

Train newcomers to perform the tasks and procedures needed for a given position.

Leader

Able to identify and develop the potential in others. Find ways to identify and leverage the strengths of others even when not readily apparent. Always on the lookout for potential leadership talent.

DEVELOPING SELF

Individual Contributor

Accountable for maintaining competence in chosen profession. Rely on support and guidance from manager/ organization to stay current with changes in your industry,

Leader

Self-development and continually adapting to change are hallmarks of success. Demonstrate initiative in pursuit of personal development. Continuously adapt to changes in markets, industry that influence success for your organization.

PROBLEM SOLVING

Individual Contributor

Like to cross problems off your list. Focus on solution and task completion. Tendency toward convergent thinking to identify solution sets. Precedence is typically a reliable guide.

Leader

Excited by problems and see them as opportunities. Divergent thinking prevails as a means to evaluate the possible options that could provide quantum leaps. Adherence to precedence can be a crutch.

COMFORT WITH AMBIGUITY

Individual Contributor

Routines and procedures are generally structured. Escalation process and rules of engagement predetermined.

Leader

Responsible for determining appropriate next steps in uncharted areas. What is or isn't allowed is significantly broader and often unclear.

NEGOTIATION

Individual Contributor

Typically will involve one-on-one situations, and matters that surround you versus others. Most often engaged with peers in this regard, or your manager. Likely to involve project scope and deadlines.

Leader

Compete for resources to devote to projects or new capabilities such as products, markets, technology, etc., requiring strong persuasive skills balanced with sound business acumen. Even disagreements about people in the business setting come back to what's best for the business. Often may involve significant financial implications (particularly when dealing with customers and expense budgets) for which you will be directly accountable.

We characterized the first summaries as having a theme of selflessness. There may not be as singular of a theme to this set, but there are a few key points that should jump out at you. First, you must thrive in the gray areas – very little of what a leader does is clear-cut, and great leaders recognize this as a creative opportunity. Second, leaders must have the ability to influence a broad spectrum of the organization – people at all levels. Third - effective leaders have an appreciation for the future. You could call this planning, but we suggest that this is too narrow a concept. Everything from people decisions to strategic plans considers a time frame independent of the present. Everybody knows what's up today – can you chart a course that sets you up for success next year? Finally, don't get in the way. You must be able to delegate effectively, and every new leader struggles with the "ask versus tell" approach to delegating as well as the helping hand. In the end, however, leaders have to be comfortable handing off the task work and standing back.

What Next?

Now that you have these tables to guide your self-analysis, you have two important points around which key career planning decisions need to be made:

1. Do you see yourself enjoying the 'working life' factors that go with a leadership role?

2. Do you believe you have the skills necessary for success in leadership?

Determining which side of the summaries appeal to you most will point you in a direction, but don't feel your results must be unanimous. There are bound to be aspects of leadership work that appeal to you more than others, and some that may outright frighten you. You may have great confidence regarding certain skills and little regarding others. In the end, if the majority of your choices seem to fall on the leader side of the preceding summaries you should consider moving forward. People may argue about whether leaders are made or born, but everybody will agree that none are perfect, and all of them struggle with different aspects of their job from time to time.

You have several resources at your disposal to help you with these decisions. Within the organization you have three 'people' resources: your manager, another member of the leadership team that you respect, and a representative from human resources. You also have work experiences from which to draw that can guide you. Resources exist outside the organization as well, and we will identify several that can be of assistance.

In an ideal world your manager will have frequent discussions with you about what you want to be when you grow up. Really good leaders will informally have this discussion several times a year outside the formal review process. These should largely revolve around observed strengths and how they can best be deployed, as well as consideration for the things that interest you most. Most importantly these talks should include an overview of what you are or can be doing to prepare for your next move. An additional aspect can and should be compensation, but it should be a secondary component unless you are starting the discussion with "What kind of work can I do that pays a lot?"

Another manager, perhaps one more senior than your direct manager, or one serving in some capacity as a mentor for you, along with somebody in human resources should also be available to have these conversations with you for added perspective. The other manager may be more familiar with other functional areas of the organization or may have experience outside the organization they can draw on in helping you think about whether or not you would be successful in a leadership role, and what you can do to better prepare for it. HR is a source for similar advice, and should offer insight into the compensation implications of whatever path you choose.

Your experience should be a powerful influence here as well. If you have an interest in leading others you should be able to put yourself in a situation where you have an informal, functional role as a leader. This can be in the form of leading a task force or committee, or maybe a significant project that's highly interdependent. These experiences can test your mettle to see if you have the raw material to be successful, and also give you a taste of a leadership experience to find out whether or not you want more. Additionally, you will have more avenues for feedback about your skills and potential as a result. If you have not yet had in informal leadership opportunity like this seek one out... that's what leaders do!

You should do yourself a favor and take advantage of resources that exist outside your organization. Let's start with a brief overview of a few published instruments – call them personality tests if you must – that are routinely used to support career path decisions. Before we open this Pandora's Box however, let me provide a health warning. <u>Test results should never be looked at as absolute data.</u> Do not base your complete "in or out" decision upon them. Rather, they are helpful supporting pieces which, when considered along with other data, can lead you to a high-quality decision. What other data? Feedback you have received from others (solicited as well as unsolicited), your performance reviews (not just the most recent one, but the general theme to you reviews over time), and the introspective journey you have no doubt taken into your own psyche. Do you like what you are doing now? Do you think you would enjoy leading people? How did you line up with the Individual Contributor versus Leader summaries in this chapter? By all means seek out an opportunity to go through one or more of these tests, but don't put undue influence on the results.

Three very popular instruments are the Myers-Briggs Type Indicator (MBTI), the DISC Profile, and the Keirsey Temperament Sorter. You will find links to web sites for these three instruments in the Manager's Toolkit at www.management-innovations.com. An additional inventory type of tool can be found by getting the book, <u>Now, Discover Your Strengths</u>, by Marcus Buckingham and Donald O. Clifton. It will link you to a tool that was developed by the Gallup Organization and is based upon their rich experience with leaders and organizations. In very simple terms, these instruments generate a high-level description of your 'type' and how it may align with various professions, including leadership roles. All three are relatively short, multiple-choice formats, with pretty straightforward questions that you can complete in less than 30 minutes. DISC and Keirsey have on-line capability but the MBTI does not. The MBTI is probably the most widely used of these three, and it is also the most involved in terms of test content and results. Somebody in your HR group may have the certification to administer the MBTI, but if not you can probably find a resource through your Employee Assistance Plan. If you are not sure if you have access to an EAP, check with human resources. In addition to accessing these instruments your EAP almost certainly includes benefits for vocational counseling, and there may be little or no cost to you for these services. We guarantee it won't cost you anything to ask, and it is difficult to estimate what it could cost you if you don't.

Another amazing resource people often overlook is their Alumni Placement Service. Even if you have a two-year degree from a Technical School or Community College, there will be an office staffed with somebody eager to help you. You may be able to leverage this concept further if there is a major university in or near the town you are working. Even if you are not an alum – offer to buy somebody in the office lunch or bring them a cup of coffee if they will give you a little of their time. These staffers universally have a wealth of counseling experience as well as an outstanding network of contacts, and, again, all you have to do is ask.

Epilogue

Resolving the "which way do I go" question is key to being at ease with your career plan, no matter which path you take. We have provided some tools to help with the decision but it is never an easy one, and it is never finished. The key here is that the path is one YOU choose, and YOU make an informed decision. There are positive attributes on both sides of this equation, the solution to which is best derived from a thoughtful, introspective exercise, perhaps with the guidance of a trusted manager. Gaining perspective of your strengths and interests from another's point of view will help assure - but not guarantee - a good decision.

In this context – for those who choose leadership roles – you will not want to cloud your mind with second thoughts once you buckle your-self into the driver's seat to lead a team. It will be vital to your success to devote 100% of your mental and emotional bandwidth to getting off on the right foot with your new team.

Discussion Questions: Pat's Dilemma

- *What would you advise Pat to do in this situation?*
- *Are Susan's weaker technical skills a concern for her ability to lead the team?*
- *Pat has only one promotion to extend. How can Pat minimize the chance of losing one of her top performers?*
- *Bob's technical skills and knowledge will make him hard to replace if he is promoted to lead the team. Should this factor into Pat's decision?*

For ideas on how the authors view the situation at Apex and Pat's Dilemma, visit the Leadership Resource Center at www.management-innovations.com, and click on Practical Lessons-Discussion Questions.

JERRY'S GREAT PLAN

Jerry Wilson grabbed his coffee cup and sprinted from his cubicle, almost late for his 10:00 a.m. meeting with Apex's CFO, Paul Burns. Jerry knew that Paul was a stickler for detail and expected his meetings to start on time and follow the agenda. He definitely didn't want to be late today, as this was the day he was going to throw his hat in the ring for the budget manager position that had been posted on the intranet yesterday.

After 45 minutes, Jerry had finished reviewing his latest project with Paul, and summoning the courage to raise the issue of the Budget Manager position, Jerry cleared his throat and launched into his pitch.

Later over lunch with his friend Ryan Bing, Jerry described how he had proceeded to trip all over himself in trying to respond to some of Paul's questions. "He said that it was good that I was interested in advancing," noted Jerry. "He asked what I was doing to prepare myself for a role like this, and he asked a lot of questions about my personal career objectives. He also wanted to know if I could describe some situations where I had used my leadership skills to help solve problems in the department," he added. "Those were all great questions, and I found that I didn't have any solid answers for Paul," lamented Jerry. "I was thankful when Rob Cushing rushed in the door with an emergency issue for Paul. I seized the moment and ran for the exit."

CHAPTER 3
LEADERSHIP—HOW DO I GET THERE FROM HERE?

You have resolved to move ahead with a leadership position, but now you wonder what it will take to get there. You know that a role won't magically drop out of the sky as a result of your personal revelation. Or at least the odds of that happening are unlikely enough that you need a better strategy than hope.

You have no doubt found yourself in the situation where somebody is working really hard to sell you something. You may have waved this person off one or two times with an impassioned "not interested" but the seller was not deterred. As you conjured up rationale after rationale for disconnecting with the process, he seemed to be armed with counter arguments that demonstrated a degree of preparation that was admirable. He probably tried to find a means to personally identify with your needs or desires. He maintained a laser-like focus in gaining your commitment. He was unflinchingly positive in his approach. This salesman has traits you must emulate to successfully move your career forward: a keen knowledge of the features and benefits of his product, a demonstrable degree of savvy for developing interpersonal relationships needed to generate leads, and a palpable passion for the product. Now it's your turn to wear the salesperson's hat – it's time to sell YOU!

From the work you did in Chapter 2, *Solo Performer or Leader*, you have a great start on creating the list of features you will highlight as part of your own sales pitch. You want to avoid the other brand comparisons and focus on what makes you a great choice. Your conviction in this regard will be genuine because you have a well thought-out rationale for why leadership is your chosen path. In this Chapter we will guide you through steps to build on that foundation and develop your own personal brand by way of a compelling career plan, steps you can take right away to market yourself and keep your momentum fueled. We'll begin with concept and insight factors, and wrap up with a recommended structure for your career plan. This plan is a powerful tool you can use for yourself as well as for those whose development you will be responsible for guiding.

Your Personal Brand

What makes you unique? Is there inherent value in you as a resource for the firm? Do you know where you want to work and why? Are you willing to accept an assignment in other functional areas of the organization to make the first step to a leadership position? Are you passionate about your subject matter expertise and want to dedicate yourself to positions that will allow you to continue to leverage that expertise? Are the answers to these questions really vital to being promoted? Yes. Much has been written about the value and importance of creating a personal brand for yourself, and that brand is what can distinguish you from the rest of the pack when selection time comes. The groundwork, however, starts now.

Personal branding has been covered by authors such as Peter Montoya and Tom Peters who compared the concept to the powerful image building of major corporations such as Motorola, Best Buy and Apple. On an individual level Peters suggests that you have a concise answer to the question "What do I do that adds remarkable, measurable, distinguished, distinctive value?" The answer to this question establishes the underpinnings of your personal marketing strategy, and a vital component of your overall career planning.

Assessing your Marketability

Where do you gather this sort of intelligence? Start with your current manager, of course. Also include the appropriate representative from human resources. Somebody in that department is a player in the process for identifying and selecting finalists for leadership roles, and you have to know where you stand with that person. Ideally, the human resource representative will have more practice assessing and recommending development activities that will enhance your viability for promotion to a leadership position. If you are in a small organization this may not be a step that is available to you. In many small firms the human resources function may be limited to compliance and record-keeping people and the more serious human resources decisions are handled by other members of management. If this is the case where you work, you will have to determine whether there is a manager at your site that wears this hat and if it appropriate to include that person in your quest for feedback. Finally, if there is an area of the organization where you have an interest but it is not your current department or under your current manager, you should have a discussion with a decision-maker in that area.

Be sensitive to the politics here – always have the first conversation with your manager, the second with human resources (assuming there is an appropriate human resource representative in your organization) and third with a manager other than your own. As part of the conversation you have with your manager you should discuss your intention to seek feedback from additional resources to round out your understanding of how competitive you are at present for leadership opportunities. Even if you don't anticipate continuing to work for your current manger -regardless of the reason- you should keep him or her informed when you talk to other managers about career opportunities. Great leaders always have a forthright sense of conviction to keep their motives visible. Or, if you prefer the cliché version, keeping all their cards on the table.

Nailing Down a Candid Assessment

In Chapter 2 we introduced a step to seek out managers for added insight about the role of a leader and your potential. If those discussions did not include the following two questions, it's time to revisit those managers and ask:

- "Do you feel I have the potential for a leadership role?"
- "Do you think I am ready now?"

Your primary objective here is to make sure you don't continually ask to be considered for promotion if the powers that be don't see you as a viable candidate. Yes, these are very direct questions, and they may make you uncomfortable when you ask them. They may make the managers uncomfortable as well. They are crucial, however, to making sure you get candid answers about your future.

If the answer to the first question is "no," the conversation should go down a different path than on to the second question. If the answer is not "yes," I am willing to bet the answer will be something uncertain rather than an absolute "no." I hate to be cynical, but even if your manager doesn't think you have this potential he or she will be reluctant to say so. I believe this is more a function of not being sufficiently trained to manage a discussion like this than evil intent or personal disregard. As we have mentioned previously, leading people is not an easy task. If the response you get is anything other than a very confident "yes" you should ask about training or development opportunities and get a commitment for a timeline to revisit this topic after you have had a chance to learn and demonstrate your manager's recommended areas of development.

When you meet with these managers make the most of the time and establish or build your relationship with them. One way to make sure you get off on the right foot when meeting with these managers is to have your pitch in order before you meet with them. You can do this by working out your first draft of your career plan before you meet so your thoughts are organized and you can begin the selling process effectively. You can practice reciting your personal value proposition (i.e. what unique qualities you have to offer) and inquiring about potential opportunities. This will help you refine your assessment of the career landscape when putting together a revised version of your plan. There are several more topics to cover, however, before we introduce the career planning worksheet at the end of this chapter.

Learn to Navigate the Internal Posting Process

If you do not consider yourself an expert on your firm's processes for posting and filling open positions then now is the time to do some research. This may be the one aspect of managing your career where subjectivity does not play a big role and a little effort spent on homework pays big dividends.

Here are questions you can use to test your knowledge of your firm's posting process. If you can't answer them succinctly take them up with your manager and/or human resources.

- Are all open positions posted in your organization?
- Is there a routine for posting openings or do they show up whenever there is a need?

- How are external candidates considered for posted positions?
- Is there a form to be completed in order to be considered?
- Who is typically involved in the screening and selection process?
- Do you know when and where postings are published?

If you are going to successfully manage your career, you want to use these processes to your advantage and not be a victim of them. Demonstrating respect for local conventions such as this will positively influence those who are involved in them. Like decision makers!

Are You Behaving Yourself?

A routine figure of speech I have used when counseling people on their career is that fairness has a long horizon, and the seeds of today's fruit were planted long ago. With that in mind, think about the following question: when is a leader not a leader? NEVER. This may seem like it is a bit of an exaggeration, but the point is you have many opportunities throughout your day to conduct yourself like a leader. You are constantly being assessed by everyone around you, and your ability to sell yourself at a later date is heavily influenced by how you act today. I recall a college class where we had an observer sit in for a few sessions before we were told she was working on a research project on leadership behavior in group settings. Everybody recognizes the instructor as the primary leader in that setting, but the fact is there were others who, through their conduct and contributions, demonstrated leadership.

Leadership behavior manifests itself in many ways during your day at work and you may not even realize it. Individual contributors display these behaviors regularly without formal leadership roles conferred on them. In our research work for this book we asked incumbent managers about identifying potential leaders, and specifically wanted to know what they heard or saw that led them to believe somebody had potential for leadership. Some interesting responses included:

- The manager received several unsolicited requests to have this person participate on committees or move to another team
- By this person's responses to problems and questions it was evident that this was somebody who was good at seeing the big picture
- She asks great questions - it began with the interview, and continues to this day. Inquisitiveness and the ability to hone in on important data will serve this person well.

- This person was outstanding with customers, and was the person I trusted to deal with difficult situations
- The way this person behaved in group settings demonstrated maturity, poise and regard for others

Art and I can occupy a day of your time with examples of behavior we have encountered that caused us to make a mental note of the person and their potential. Here are a few for your consideration:

- Being the first to speak; volunteering when others hesitate. When something unpopular or undesirable needs to be done, or there is risk and uncertainty in the air, leaders forge ahead. There seems to be an innate willingness to take the risk of being wrong that is balanced with a desire to move ahead.

- Expressing support for inclusion versus exclusion. Has everybody in the group overtly been asked to contribute if they haven't already? When you speak up in favor of including others in the fact-finding, communication, problem solving, etc. you are being a leader. Too often people tend to lean toward exclusion as an easier path or because there are people they don't like and don't want to hear from.

- Having the confidence to express a contrary opinion. This may happen as much for encouraging richness in debate as true disagreement with the prevailing thought. Demonstrating and encouraging critical thinking is a strong leadership virtue.

- Demonstrating a sense of self-awareness. This can include everything from your voice and tone (always using your outside voice in the office will disenfranchise everybody) to balancing how much they participate in group settings. True leaders don't always have to be out front but they step forward when the situation warrants.

- Having a prevailing positive, can-do attitude. How many times have you heard or been part of a discussion about a troublesome team member that is summarized as "they have a bad attitude?" The behavioral scientist in me hates such a vague generalization of behavior. On the other hand, the manager in me relishes the spirit of those we characterize as having a great attitude. The glass is ALWAYS half-full, and just imagine what you might get into the other half.

These illustrations make a case that promoting managers benefit from what may initially seem like indirect cues when identifying and assessing potential leaders. You are now armed with several examples which, if demonstrated, will help you be seen as a leader independent of applying for openings when they occur and give you a leg up on those who may just 'hang paper' when a posting appears. Keep in mind that you are always 'on display' and under the constant scrutiny of others beyond your immediate boss and peers. The way you carry yourself at all times has a profound impact on decision makers' assessment of your capability and potential for a leadership position. The opportunity to create favorable impressions is in your hands, and represents the first step on your campaign trail.

Promoting Yourself Before the Promotion

If you are already showing the traits of a leader as you go through your daily routine, you probably want something more digestible as a next step in blazing your personal trail to a leadership position. These include challenges where you can be assigned a formal leadership role minus the direct reporting relationships. The beauty in these opportunities is they often carry a phenomenal cost-benefit ratio, a great deal of experience and visibility with no out of pocket expense. More importantly, they underscore your career interest in being a leader and showcase your initiative. Let's review some of the opportunities you can find.

- **Compelling Projects:** There may be an important initiative for your team, department or organization that needs a leader or project manager. Volunteer! It doesn't get any more straightforward than this.

- **Broad Organizational Initiatives:** Perhaps your firm is preparing or updating their strategic plan. Maybe a cultural change initiative? Even if you can't get a role leading a portion of one of these projects, get involved somehow. This experience will sharpen your business skills and probably give you a chance to learn something about the business.

- **Process Improvement:** If your department is implementing a new reporting or recordkeeping system, there will be an opportunity to map and redesign critical business processes. If you are not in the throes of a process improvement project in a formal way, ask to take one on. There is always something that can be done more effectively. Probably many things. Even more enticing for management, there may be something that can be eliminated that is not adding value. Again, an opportunity to develop your business skill as well as knowledge of the operation

- **Research Projects:** These could cover innovating anything from new technology to new product development. If you are not directly involved in those things in your present role it shouldn't preclude your involvement now, especially if you ask nice. Also be prepared to invest your own time for a research project if you can't find a formal opportunity to work on something. Either way, research projects allow you to exercise your creativity and open-mindedness.

- **Train and Mentor Others:** This may be the perfect way to jump-start your formal leadership experience. In these situations the results you will be accountable for will mirror the things you will be responsible for as the assigned leader. As anybody that has been a tutor will tell you, it also solidifies your understanding of the subject matter – it's difficult to show somebody the ropes if you don't know them.

- **Fill in for Your Manager:** Many organizations have a routine where managers who will be absent identify a stand-in. This may involve being the manager on duty while your manager is on vacation or attending a meeting if your manager has a scheduling conflict. In my experience the substitute may be either the likely successor or the duty is rotated amongst people a level below the manager. The underlying motive is the same in either case – give those with the potential to be promoted some time in the game.

    Be warned: I can tell you I have seen the stand-in treated like a substitute teacher –tested by the team and the "regular teachers." The behavior here is interesting to watch as a barometer of acceptance. Aside from the ribbing (which is to be expected) you can tell if there is underlying respect for the substitute's candidacy as a future member of the leadership team. If your organization doesn't have the stand-in practice in place now, ask your manger if you can start it. That's what a leader would do.

As much as I love using quotes to reinforce a point, I don't know who deserves credit for saying "there is no time like the present" but I hope you can appreciate how it applies here. If you can start acting like a leader today or tomorrow, why wait?

Personal Development 202

You have an opportunity to be creative here – some opportunities for development may not be readily apparent but they are there. Be open to what's going on outside your four walls as a way to expand the universe of development options. Small and mid-sized companies will often have limited resources for leadership training, but no matter where you find yourself, a little divergent thinking about the possibilities can go a long way in achieving your personal development objectives. Let's look at a few creative ideas for development opportunities.

- Ask about creating a training cycle for aspiring managers if one is not already in place. Perhaps an existing program for managers can be retooled with little time, effort or expense for aspiring leaders. This is a golden opportunity to work on your analytical and influence skills. Can you make a case for your organization to invest in such a program? Can you get the powers to be to act on that analysis?

- A number of seminars are offered to the public at large, many geared toward leadership development. Some may focus on applied skills, others on concepts and philosophies of leadership. Odds are somebody in your organization already receives mailing promotions for these seminars so ask around. The cost for these can range from a couple hundred dollars to a several thousand depending on location, duration and the organization offering the seminar. A general rule of thumb is that better programs cost more than lower quality programs, but you should always check out the content and the source before you commit. There are some really weak programs out there. If it costs less than $100 per day you should probably skip it. National training entities such as the American Management Association are a safe bet, as are offerings from premier four-year universities with a reputation for graduate management degree and executive/continuing education programs. A final source for external leadership development programs is your professional association. Many national associations offer programs that balance leadership and management skill development with updating domain expertise.

- Volunteer for a community service project. The range of possibilities is endless – from faith-based groups to social service agencies to youth sports. As you may have learned from prior experience, there are opportunities to lead for anybody willing to step up.

Leading volunteers is a tremendous challenge and will be a great way to hone your organizational skills and energy level.

- You may also find that there is a community based leadership development program in your area in which you can participate. You local chamber of commerce or community college can put you in touch with such a program if it is available. An added benefit of these programs is you can develop contacts with whom you can network on your learning experiences. Contacts from outside your company will obviously add variety to your bag of tricks since they are dealing with a different universe of people and circumstances.

If the expense is a prohibitive factor with your firm please think about paying for the program yourself. Perhaps you can split it with your organization. If you pay for the program will the company will pick up the business expense (hotel, travel, etc.) if any, or give you the time off so you don't have to burn vacation? I hesitate to suggest the individual should bear any of this cost, but if times are tough where you work this may be the only solution. Think about it from this perspective: who really loses if you stand on principle and refuse to assume some or all of the expense associated with your development?

Finally, there is an interesting conclusion we drew from research participants who often suggested that new leaders benefited greatly from the opportunity to spend time with other leaders. It stands to reason that aspiring leaders can also benefit from this. It can be as simple as a roundtable-like brown bag luncheon where experienced leaders share current challenges in leading people and the business or discuss recent books and article they have read, to something more formal such as presentations from experienced leaders on topics such as leadership characteristics valued by the firm. If conventions like these don't currently exist it's an opportunity for enterprising, aspiring - and experienced - leaders to get them started.

Your Career Plan

Odds are that you have not had the benefit of collaborating with your manager to establish a career plan. Our research work suggests that not only is the planning step lacking in most organizations, but the decision-making for an individual's career is influenced more by the firm than the individual. We're going to help you break that cycle. We've come to the point where you will corral the material in the first three chapters and convert it to energy in the form of your personal career plan.

This is a situation where a great tool will compel you to first think broadly about your career possibilities, then utilize input and guidance from others, and finally catalyze your thinking in the form of a powerful rationale, well-reasoned goals and actionable steps. Sometimes we believe we have a great idea until the time comes to commit it to writing and we realize it's not as strong as we had hoped. You don't want to take that chance when it comes to your career. Answer these questions as honestly and specifically as you can and you will greatly increase the likelihood of getting to where you want to go. In the Manager's Toolkit at our website: www.management-innovations.com you will find these questions in the form of a downloadable *Career Planning Worksheet* that will guide you in creating your written plan.

Career Planning Questions

1. **What is your personal value proposition?** Describe it in terms of the unique skills and attributes you have to offer. If you are specifically seeking leadership roles refer to the material in Chapter 2 as a guide.

2. **What is your career vision?** Describe your ultimate career objective, giving primary consideration to the role versus a specific position or title (e.g. Head of National Field Sales versus Senior Sales Manager at Mullarkey Corp; Company President versus President of the Metals Group at ArtRich Enterprises). You may, however, want to focus on a particular industry (e.g. software, manufacturing, retail, not-for-profits, etc.)

   a. Why will this position be rewarding for you?

   b. What does it take to be successful in this position and how do you compare at this point in time?

   c. Summarize the development you will need, and identify the likely source (e.g. work experience, formal training programs, specific skills, etc.)

   d. Identify a likely path (progression of positions) to your ultimate objective along with a time frame.

      i. Is there a preferred path and an alternate path?

      ii. Is there a traditional path that others in the ultimate objective role have taken?

      iii. Are you willing to assume a role outside of your area of functional expertise or experience?

3. **Is your environment conducive to your ultimate goal?**

   a. Have you considered opportunities that may exist beyond your team, department and functional area? If so, what are they?

   b. Does your ultimate goal position exist in your current organization?

   c. Is your current organization in your preferred industry?

   d. Do you anticipate promotion activity to the extent that opportunities may reasonably materialize? If not, what is your plan to avoid being stuck?

   e. Can you expect a commitment to make development activities available as needed to meet your objectives? If not, what are you prepared to do about your development needs?

4. **In consideration of your ultimate goal and preferred path, what is your best next opportunity?**

   a. What is your contingency plan if the opportunity for your next best step doesn't materialize?

   b. What lateral opportunities could also benefit you from a development standpoint?

5. **Who are the influential managers you will contact to promote interest in your aspirations?**

   a. Who are those who will have an impact on your ultimate goal?

   b. Who are the ones who will have influence on your more immediate goals?

6. **What initiatives will you undertake in the next twelve months to make the next step in your career plan?**

   a. Identify personal development, coaching and project assignments

   b. What support do you expect from others in this pursuit?

7. **What feedback have you received about your plan?**

   a. When you look over your answers and ideas above, are you excited about your plan and prospects? If not, change them accordingly.

    b.   Include peers that you work with and who you believe will be candid. They see you in action on a daily basis and know you as well as anyone.

    c.   Seek guidance on your plan from your manager, other managers that you respect and those who will be in a position to support your plan.

    d.   Consider adjustments to your plan based on the feedback received.

8. **Do you understand the triggers for revisiting your plan?**

    a.   Has it been more than two years since you last updated your plan?

    b.   Have you changed positions or companies since you last updated your plan?

It may seem like a daunting task to complete this plan but think of it as analogous to a car's GPS system. Those marvels of graphics and mapping are totally useless for getting you where you want to go without a specific destination plugged into them. Much like the auto industry incrementally adopting these systems to the point they become standard equipment, organizations will gradually recognize the need to identify and develop leaders as a key competency for survival. Until then it will be incumbent on you to pull over, break out the paper version, and figure things out the old fashioned way.

Some Final Thoughts on Your Career Plan

Don't feel you are tied to your plan once you develop it. You should expect that it will evolve and those around you will also expect it to evolve. You change; business changes; opportunities change. Don't let the potential for this kind of change hinder your thought process – have an idea for where you want to end up and what roles you believe will best prepare you for that ultimate goal. Revisit and refresh it as conditions change so it is always current.

As we have mentioned elsewhere, careers are defined as much by lateral movement – meaning moves at or near your current level, but perhaps in a different department, category or functional area – as by vertical movement. Don't overlook lateral opportunities to learn more about your operation and the people engaged there as a means to your end. Often times the path to a desired role will be through another position. There are worse things than only having one step in mind at a time, but your sales pitch will be much more compelling if you can articulate how the current position about which you are expressing interest fits into your overall career objectives.

Finally, once it's developed don't keep your plan locked in the safe. Share what you have to offer with others. Read up on networking and unleash the power it has for making connections and learning. You will discover how miraculously you can market yourself without really trying. What does that mean? I'm not going to tell you - it's *your* career, go read a book! (*HINT: you can find references on networking in the Reading List section of the Management Innovations website at* www.management-innovations.com.)

Epilogue

Great leaders always believe there is something they can do when faced with a problem. It is too easy to stop in your tracks when you meet an obstacle, but that isn't the kind of approach either of your authors condone. As an eager, aspiring leader, it may seem like you have an insurmountable challenge to stand out from the pack when everybody is waving his or her hand for a turn at the wheel. Think of this inflection point as a prime opportunity to demonstrate your own creativity and initiative in the form of your personal branding campaign. There is always something you can do. This is a mission-critical concept for those of you who have leadership in your blood but don't yet have a formal opportunity to lead.

I heard one of the most profound leadership parables from Art. Not from school or a book. It is based on a Star Trek movie. It involves the Kobayashi Maru – a renowned, unsolvable training exercise from the Star Fleet Academy. In this exercise, the Kobayashi Maru is a fictional starship in which command trainees are presented with a no-win battle scenario as a test of character. This simulation is legend amongst academy graduates for eliciting frustration and bringing out the worst in them. To make things worse, nobody has ever negotiated a successful outcome, but they all keep trying. A young James Kirk takes it upon himself to secretly reprogram the rules of the game in the computer that controls the exercise so a winning scenario is possible. Of course the academy was not pleased with Kirk's end-around tactic, but they had to admire the approach: if a solution doesn't exist, rethink the problem and develop a plan accordingly. Your own career plan… that's what great leaders do, and you can start now!

LEADERSHIP—HOW DO I GET THERE FROM HERE?

Discussion questions: Jerry's great plan.

- *How could Jerry have better managed the meeting with Paul?*
- *Was Paul out of line for asking the questions that he did?*
- *If you were Paul, what would you do to help Jerry prepare for a promotion to a leadership role?*

For ideas on how the authors view the situation at Apex and the issues outlined above, visit the Leadership Resource Center at www.management-innovations. com, and click on Practical Lessons-Discussion Questions.

PART TWO
SUCCEEDING FROM THE START

PREFACE TO CHAPTER 4

SUSAN GETS THE NOD

Driving home on Friday afternoon, Susan Smith was ecstatic. She had just learned from Pat Paulsen, her manager that she had earned the promotion to Customer Support Supervisor. Susan felt like she had just won a big prize. She truly had not thought she would be selected over Bob Hobson, the resident technical genius, but apparently Pat was impressed with the team activities that Susan had led over the past year. Susan knew that this was an important step in her career, and for the first time ever, the drive home on a Friday had her wishing it were Monday morning.

Pat prepares for Susan

Susan wasn't the only one to drive home with a smile on her face. Pat was relieved that she had made a decision about the support supervisor position. She felt good about Susan's potential, and it seemed like Bob Hobson, the other candidate, was not too upset about the outcome.

Relieved that this problem had been resolved, Pat began thinking about what she needed to do to help Susan with her new role. She thought about her first job as a manager and cringed at some of the missteps she had made in her first year. "If only I could help Susan avoid those problems and focus on improving our customer support services, we would be much better off," thought Pat. She made a note to jot down her ideas on avoiding common first-time manager missteps over the weekend and to speak with Susan before the public announcement of the promotion on Monday. As she turned into her driveway, her thoughts moved to her weekend plans.

Susan finds a Peer

Mark Ackman was two weeks into his role as manager for the eastern region telemarketing team. His excitement over the promotion had dulled by noon on his first day after accepting the resignation from his star performer, watching helplessly as another employee cried in his office, and completely bungling his first staff meeting.

Mark bumped into Susan on the way out and offered his congratulations on the promotion. He also warned her to be ready for the unexpected. Susan asked if they could get together for lunch next week and compare notes, and maybe help each other out in their new roles and Mark readily agreed. They made plans to meet next Wednesday at 12:30 p.m.

CHAPTER 4
THE TOP TEN CHALLENGES THAT YOU FACE AS A (NEW) LEADER

My initial intention for this chapter was to provide the first-time leader with advance warning of the most common mistakes that he or she is likely to make during their first few years in a management role. Imagine if someone were to come up to you on your first day of your first management job and indicate that they could predict with remarkable accuracy, all of the major leadership challenges that you would face over the next year or two. While it might sound too good to be true, hopefully, you would jump at the opportunity to learn about the issues so that you could deftly navigate them on your leadership journey. And while this is still the intent of this chapter, there was one flaw in my initial thinking. The top ten obstacles that we will explore in the next few pages do not discriminate between new or experienced leaders. They are equal opportunity obstacles.

The focus of this chapter is to help you understand and anticipate the most common challenges that a leader faces in establishing their role with a new team. It does not matter whether you are a grizzled veteran of the leadership world, or a first-time manager, you will need to recognize and deal with these challenges in each and every role. Unlike the remainder of the book, which offers up detailed solutions to these and other leadership challenges, this chapter is about recognition. As I look back on my own career, I truly wish someone had sat down with me and pointed out where I was likely to misstep. This heads-up would have saved me a number of misfires, and allowed me to increase my contribution to my employers. With this chapter and this book, you gain the benefit of my 20:20 leadership hindsight.

A Word to Promoting Managers

As a manager charged with the task of developing others, you have a unique opportunity to help aspiring professionals understand the realities of leading and the obstacles that they will face along the way. You can be that manager that takes the time to help people sort out whether leadership is right for them, and if so, you have a unique opportunity to prepare them for their future. Chances are, no one took the time to help you make an educated decision on your leadership career, much less highlight where the missteps and mistakes were likely to occur. You should not repeat this same mistake. If you accept that the most important thing that you can do in your career is positively impact someone's career and life, then leverage the content in this book and in this chapter to good effect. As I stated above, I wish that the leaders that I worked for had the foresight and presence of mind to know that helping me anticipate where I might go awry would help me become a more effective and productive leader. If you did not receive this counsel, then you have all the more reason to do things differently with your associates. If you are one of the fortunate few that worked for someone that truly served as a leadership mentor, then pay it forward.

The Top Ten Challenges

As a leader, you are in the people management business. Unfortunately, people are remarkably difficult to manage. There is no single formula or approach that you can apply to ensure that people are happy, motivated, trusting, honest, inspired and committed to your cause or the cause of your organization. There are however, many mistakes that you can make that will turn them against you. The *Top Ten* are all people issues that you will encounter over and over again during your career, so you would be wise to study them carefully, to anticipate them as you move into new roles, and to pay close attention to the rest of the book as we develop the tools and approaches to help you knock them down one at a time.

THE TOP TEN CHALLENGES

#1- *People do not naturally want to be led by you*

It may come as a shock, but no one is particularly interested in working for YOU. A promotion and a title might bestow grudging tolerance and even a little bit of deference, but never credibility or true respect. Until you have proven yourself as someone that has integrity, and is focused on doing the right things for people and for the business, don't expect the troops to be lining up outside your door to sign on with your team.

Earning the respect of your team is one of the most difficult tasks for a new leader. Your team is judging your every word and every action, looking for inconsistencies or for a clue to your "real" agenda. They are also looking for reasons to trust you as their leader, and you need to supply those reasons.

Most new managers don't understand that the best way to earn credibility is through proving their integrity—making certain that their agenda is visible, that their words and actions always match, and that their intentions are noble. Ultimately, your credibility is your currency as a leader, and if you focus on building and reinforcing it, you will prosper.

#2- *Everyone has an agenda...they just don't always share it*

New leaders like to believe that everyone looks at business challenges, departmental objectives and initiatives from the same perspective—theirs. They work to communicate goals and objectives, to "get everyone on the same page," and if they are really clear and persistent, they might even begin to hear their own words echo back through the words of their team. Sounds like success, right? Wrong! This manager dramatically underestimates how diverse and divergent people's agendas, ambitions, interests and motivations truly are. As a new leader, the only way to move beyond superficial conversation to the real issues confronting the team and the business, is to develop the ability to ask the right questions; listen to what people mean, not what they say; and become an astute observer of interactions. Your advanced degree in human psychology will be remarkably useful for this part of your job. Lacking that degree, welcome to the world of mere managerial mortals, and realize that you need to learn how to truly pay attention to your associates.

#3-The personal problems of your associates will become your problems if you let them (and sometimes you can't help it).

New managers and some experienced leaders attract their staff's personal problems like flowers attract bees. You will find yourself on the receiving end of people's challenges in their personal lives, with their health, their finances, their romances, their children and just about every other dilemma that humans encounter. Performance issues will become blurred by personal challenges and your initial reaction will either be to empathize too much or too little, thus creating the next layer of the problem…one that is now yours. Depending upon your approach, some individuals may attempt to manipulate you using their personal issues as a lever. Since as we discussed before, your every action is being watched and judged by your charges, your handling of these circumstances with one individual will have a ripple effect through the rest of your team, impacting your credibility, perceived integrity and potentially the team's results.

Navigating this particularly sticky obstacle will require you to establish an approach for keeping everyone's focus on business, ensuring an environment of fairness and maintaining your humanity as people deal with legitimate challenges in their lives. Ultimately, the people side of people management is a delicate art form that takes time, experience and perspective to do well.

#4-Your instinct says, "Do it my way because I'm the boss." Your instinct is wrong.

One of the interesting wake-up moments for a new leader is the first time that someone voices disagreement with their opinion or direction. It is shocking, embarrassing and remarkably uncomfortable for the leader that feels compelled to defend their position. At this point, it is tempting to play the, "I'm in charge" card, asserting authority and superiority. After all, the leader was promoted to lead. They're in charge and of course their opinion must be correct. Right? Wrong!

It takes time, self-confidence and insight into what your true role as a leader is all about to realize that the assertion of, "I'm in charge," or, "Because I said so," is best left for your parenting chores and checked at the door when you enter the office. In fact, you will come to value alternative viewpoints and people that have the confidence to voice their opinions, including their disagreement with you. Your ability to create an environment that facilitates productive debate and problem solving is critical to your success as a leader.

#5-It takes time to learn and internalize the parable of, "The Scorpion and the Frog."

A scorpion approaches a frog and asks the frog to let him ride on his back across the pond. The frog responds appropriately with, "Why would I do that? You are a scorpion and I know that as I am swimming with you on my back across the pond, you will sting me and we will both die." The scorpion answers convincingly, "I certainly won't do that. I've changed. I really want to get across the pond, and if I sting you, we will both die." The frog thinks about it awhile and agrees that it makes no sense for the scorpion to do that. Perhaps he really has changed. Finally, he says, "Ok, jump on and I will take you to the other side." Halfway across the pond, the scorpion stings the frog and with his dying gasp, the frog asks, "Why did you do that? I though you said you changed." With no hesitation, the scorpion responds, "I'm a scorpion. It's my nature to sting. What did you expect?"

The moral for the new leader: you will likely spend an inordinate amount of time attempting to change people, or worse yet, providing people who have convinced you that they've changed, with too much latitude. You will delay tough personnel decisions in the belief that people will change their behaviors, not realizing that these behaviors are driven by their nature. Of course, your intentions are noble—almost humanistic. It's too bad your intentions are wrong.

Navigating this obstacle requires you to understand your business priorities, to work hard on aligning the right talent and skill sets with the right challenges, and perhaps most importantly, to have the self confidence to conduct the tough discussions that are necessary to provide people with the opportunity to change or to move them on to their next career outside your firm.

#6-We all have weaknesses, don't make them your focal point.

Similar to challenge number five, you will be tempted to focus your developmental efforts and guidance around people's weaknesses versus improving their strengths. This is one of my favorite obstacles, because it is so easy to fall into the trap, and in fact many of our corporate customs, including performance reviews provided by naïve but well intentioned human resources departments require you to call out weaknesses and suggest developmental plans. It is easy to focus on the fact that someone might stink at public speaking, but be a brilliant contributor in other ways. Your instinct will be to solve their public speaking problem through assignments, courses or readings, when in reality you should be focusing on ways to better leverage and develop the areas where they show brilliance. Of course, if public speaking is fundamental to either their job or their development as a professional, I will grudgingly agree that it merits some investment in time.

Remember, it is not your responsibility to fix the flaws of your associates. Learn to leverage people's strengths and develop teams where the members have complementary skills, and you will succeed beyond your wildest dreams.

#7-The key to leading people is obvious. Too bad that no one will tell you what it is.

No one that is, except me. The answer is, "Respect." The same lesson that your parents and teachers taught you in your childhood..."treat others as you would like to be treated," applies here. Everyone has basic needs, and once we move up a few rungs on Maslow's ladder, things like being treated with respect and dignity are extremely important. Your willingness to invest in someone, to provide them an opportunity to take a risk and fail or succeed and your time investment to pay attention to what and how they are doing, all contribute to you showing respect for your team member.

Unfortunately, you will run across too many leaders that do not understand how important it is to treat others with respect. These leaders seem to feel a compulsion to assert their authority and superiority at the expense of people's dignity. They gain compliance at the end of a metaphorical gun barrel, driving people with fear and intimidation. They also learn to watch their backs, because the list of people interested in their leadership demise is long.

The theme of "treating people with respect" is inherent in everything we write about in this book, and in everything that we believe in about effective leadership. There are few absolutes in life, but this is one of them.

#8-The most important part of your job is probably not in your job description

Creating the effective work environment is your real job. Whether your title says manager, supervisor or vice-president, your basic mission is the same: to create a working environment that fosters operational excellence and a spirit of innovation. This is a difficult task that takes time, your commitment and a dose of humility to recognize that the most important thing that you can do is create an environment where your day to day involvement is almost inconsequential to your team's great performance.

Many leaders never realize the importance of the work environment, their responsibility for shaping it, nor do they understand the signs that indicate whether it's working or failing. These tend to be the command and control leaders that feel compelled to insert themselves into every situation and assert their right to decide at all times. They don't realize the impact that their approach has on the work environment, and they lack the self-confidence to let their subordinates make decisions and take risks. You have an opportunity to do it the right way. Don't let your ego keep you from becoming a great leader.

#9 Beware over-investing your time and energy with the wrong people

Analogous to the challenges you will face in over-investing in fixing people's weaknesses or in relearning the story of the Scorpion and the Frog over and over again, will be the headache of dealing with the brilliant problem-child employee. You will be tempted to either rationalize away the problematic portion of their involvement or you will invest an inordinate amount of energy in trying to get these talented but difficult individuals to change or eliminate their aberrant behaviors. You will send them to programs, provide extraordinary amounts of time and energy on coaching and likely bludgeon them with review content that says, "Joel is a remarkable talent with a tremendous impact on our business. However, his inability to function effectively as part of a team..." You will work harder for these people than any others, and they will be the single biggest source of your frustration.

I have managed a number of these individuals during my career, and the story is consistent from person to person. The individual displays outstanding technical skills and is vocal about their desire to advance in their career. Early on, you see the blemishes and issues, but push them aside due to the technical brilliance that the person displays. As the issues begin to impact others on the team, you begin coaching on an incident-by-incident basis. The annual performance review provides you with an opportunity to formally call the person on the carpet, and armed by their commitment to "do better," you assume that the problem is solved. Unfortunately, the cycle will start all over again.

These brilliant problem-children lack the emotional intelligence to recognize their aberrant behaviors, and therefore rarely if ever change. You perpetuate this vicious cycle by maintaining and supporting these people, even when all of the signs say to cut them loose. These projects nearly always end in failure and will scar you more than any other missteps in your career. The solution to this complex obstacle is to learn to recognize this brilliant problem-child and to develop a program that incorporates reasonable efforts, but that has a defined beginning, end and possible outcomes. Your HR resources are critical to helping you over this obstacle and your ability to conduct the tough discussions as outlined in chapter nine is essential. Failure to overcome this obstacle will slow you down and dramatically reduce the effectiveness of you and your team.

#10-You are responsible for your team's results.

At the end of the day, you only have to look in the mirror to see who is responsible for the results of your team. The fact that you are a new leader, or that you took over a team in shambles is interesting but irrelevant. The day that you walk in the door as leader of a team, you assume responsibility for all of the outcomes. It is your responsibility to ensure that you and your team understand their mission in supporting a firm's strategy, that you have the right people in the right roles working on the right priorities, and that you are doing everything you can to develop an effective work environment. As the saying goes, it's your name on the door and you are accountable. It's not pleasant to feel the cold hand of reality slapping you across the face, but then again it's real life.

A Word to New and Aspiring Leaders

During the review process for this book a particularly talented new manager commented upon reading this chapter, "Now I'm scared. I knew my job was going to be tough, but I don't know how I will get through all of these challenges." She also indicated words to the effect that an aspiring leader reading this chapter might be frightened away from a first management job. As context, this individual is a rising star in their organization and had recently been promoted from within to lead a group of peers in a highly technical function. From our questioning, it appeared that she was doing the right things right, building credibility, establishing operating procedures and working through the challenge of being the leader over her former group of peers.

Rich and I were pleased in one sense that we had elicited recognition on the difficulty and challenges of leading, but concerned that we would turn off aspiring leaders too early in the process. As we have said numerous times, leading effectively is hard work. In the words of another of our reviewers, "Leadership is a profession with a body of knowledge waiting to be discovered by the practitioner." We truly believe that leadership is a profession and that like any other, it should be approached with eyes wide open about the challenges and rewards, and the commitment required for success.

If you are an aspiring or a new leader reading these pages and you find yourself questioning whether you have made the right choice, you probably have. It is the wise and committed person that knows what they are up against and perseveres in spite of their knowledge of the obstacles. None of the challenges and issues that we describe are insurmountable, and in fact with the approaches and guidance, combined with your passion for leading, they are eminently solvable. On the other hand, if all you were looking for from a role in leadership was an office with a door, a bigger paycheck and the license to dictate your direction, perhaps you should reconsider.

PRACTICAL LESSONS IN LEADERSHIP

THE SHORT-FORM:

The Top Ten Challenges of the New Leader

#1- People do not naturally want to be led by you
First, prove your credibility and earn their respect.

#2-Everyone has an agenda...they just don't always share it
Learn to truly pay attention to your associates.

#3-The personal problems of your associates will become your problems if you let them
Learn to keep the focus on business and remember to be a human being.

#4-Your instinct says, "Do it my way because I'm the boss." Your instinct is wrong.
Success comes when you realize that "you" are not the subject.

#5-It takes time to learn and internalize the parable of, "The Scorpion and the Frog."
Recognize that people do not change their nature,

#6-We all have weaknesses, don't make them your focal point.
Play to the strengths and complement the weaknesses.

#7-The key to leading people is obvious. Too bad that no one will tell you what it is.
Respect.

#8-The most important part of your job is probably not in your job description
You are responsible for creating the effective work environment.

#9 Beware over-investing your time and energy with the wrong people
Be fair and be decisive.

#10-You are responsible for your team's results.
You are accountable.

Epilogue

As I stated at the opening, you will face these *Top Ten Challenges* repeatedly during your career. The names will change, the companies will be different, but these common challenges will always be present to remind you how tough it is to be an effective leader. It might be tempting to sidestep the difficult issues, but it is never the right thing to do. When you signed on to be a leader, you implicitly agreed that you would step up and work through these problems with the utmost integrity, respect for your associates and commitment to your organization to do the right thing at all times. I've never seen a leader that bypassed the tough issues succeed in more than the short-term. Don't fall into the trap of thinking that there is an easy way out for a tough problem. There are no shortcuts.

Discussion questions-Susan Gets the Nod

- *What should Susan be thinking about as she prepares for Monday?*
- *What should Pat's role be in guiding Susan during her start-up?*
- *How can Mark and Susan help each other?*
- *What would you put on Susan's '60 Day To-Do' list?*

For ideas on how the authors view the situation at Apex and the issues outlined above, visit the Leadership Resource Center at www.management-innovations. com, and click on Practical Lessons-Discussion Questions.

PREFACE TO CHAPTER 5

SUSAN'S FIRST DAY

"Well, that went pretty well," thought Susan as she accepted the last of the congratulations from her new team and followed them out of the conference room. Pat Paulsen, Susan's manager had introduced Susan as the new support supervisor, and judging by the reaction on people's faces, it was a good choice. Even Bob Hobson, the other internal candidate for the job had shaken her hand and indicated that he was looking forward to working together. "Not bad at all," thought Susan as she savored the moment while walking through the door of her new office.

By 4:30 p.m. that afternoon, the happy thoughts following the morning's announcement meeting had given way to a whole new range of emotions. Susan wasn't sure if it was shock, panic, fear or some combination of the above. It had all started within 15 minutes of her sitting at her new desk, and it was downhill from there.

First it was the visit from Jerry Wilson in finance. Jerry explained that although she was new in the job, it was budget time, and he needed numbers from her by Thursday afternoon. "Doable," she thought. Then, the update meeting on the new customer relationship management software deployment indicated that there were some snags and in order to hit the beginning of the quarter target, Susan would have to make some big priority calls right away. After that, she had her first encounter as supervisor with an irate customer complaining of the poor service and even poorer attitude expressed by one of her employees. After that, her lunch was interrupted by one her employees, Rob Curtiss, who informed her that he was thinking of leaving because he was being grossly underpaid. And to top it all off, her first staff meeting seemed more like an organized street fight, with staffers arguing over nearly every idea and issue.

When Mark Ackman stuck his head in the door just before 5:00 p.m. to see how she was doing, she looked at him and said, "Mark, I think we need to do lunch sooner than Wednesday. What are you doing tomorrow?" she asked.

CHAPTER 5
CONGRATULATIONS, YOU HAVE
A TEAM! NOW WHAT?

Your first day with your first team is one of the most exciting and frightening days of your career. Your excitement about the new position is likely exceeded by the uncertainty that you feel over what to expect. How will your new team react to you? What does your boss really expect from you? How do you get people to follow your direction? Does this tie go with this jacket? I've known people that have changed clothes three times before they could get out of the house and head for work on their first day of a management job. And while there is no proof that your choice of day one outfit or that matching just the right tie with the right jacket will impact your success, clearly, you want everything to be just right.

If you are an experienced manager, you might not have as much trouble dressing on the first day of a new leadership role, but it is likely that you feel the butterflies swirling as well. You have some experience with the start-up process, but you also know that you have a lot work ahead of you to win over a new team and begin to make the changes that your boss hired you to make.

Whether you are brand new to management or an experienced veteran, it is essential that by the time you walk in the door on day one you have a game plan in place for the first few months of this important start-up phase. I have learned through experience and trial and error that start-up is too important to leave to chance, and I always show up with a game plan that maps out how I am going to get to know my team, how I will get a handle on the business issues and market conditions, and what I will do to begin building my leadership credibility. While there are always some unexpected surprises and new learning experiences along the way, the process for starting up with a new team is similar from company to company and function to function whether you are a first time manager or a new CEO.

I confess that I love the start-up phase of a new leadership role more than anything else in business. It is filled with fresh challenges, new people and new experiences and it is a period rich in learning and problem solving. After doing this many times during two decades of work for both large and small organizations, I approach the start-up phase of a new job with the confidence borne from experience that I will succeed, regardless of the situation. I know that I need to understand my business mission, establish myself as a credible leader, leverage my team for input and guidance while assessing their talent, and finally, make some tough decisions that will impact the careers of a number of people. And while there is a fine line between confidence and arrogance that one should never cross, my own self-assurance comes from having a game plan in place to begin to understand the people, issues, the core mission and potential solutions. Arrogant would be thinking that I know all of the answers. Confident is having a plan to pursue the answers. In fact, when starting in a new role, I don't know most of the answers, but by following the script that we will develop in this chapter, it does not take long before the answers become clear to all parties.

The Importance of an Effective Start-up

At the risk of stating the obvious, you get a chance to be the new leader just once in every position, and it is essential to use this early phase effectively to build a foundation for future success. Gone are the days of a honeymoon period where the new leader was given an unspecified amount of time to acclimate to the new job and surroundings. Instead, today's leaders work in an environment characterized by a remarkable rate of change, fierce global competition and the constant threat of disruption from new competitors and technologies. The expectations, right or wrong, are that everyone, including the new leader, is doing everything possible to drive results, serve customers and beat the competition. And while it takes time to affect change, transform a team or move in a new direction, a strong foundation, built on the leader's credibility and ability to understand and translate the business mission into meaningful action, is essential to success.

The New Leader's Vision and Purpose

The most effective leaders are guided by a strong sense of purpose and a vision for what they need to accomplish to realize their vision. This sense of purpose and the vision are formed through the leader's focus on four critical start-up tasks. And while there are seemingly endless things for the new leader to invest his or her time in, it is essential that everything tie back to these four priorities.

Four Primary Start-up Tasks for the New Leader

1. Understand the business mission of your team
2. Get to know your team and let them get to know you
3. Begin to build your leadership credibility
4. Understand what everyone on your team is doing

If you successfully focus on these issues, you will build a foundation of knowledge to begin directing the business priorities of your team as well as build the personal relationships that will be essential to successfully identifying and implementing changes. And while these four tasks seem straightforward, take a look at your calendar and your to-do list after your first few days on the job. It is likely that both will be filled with urgent and unimportant meetings and tasks, most of which have nothing to do with the four start-up priorities. It's time to rearrange your to-do list.

Armed with an understanding of your four primary tasks and forewarned of some insidious progress inhibitors that we will detail later in the chapter, you will be well prepared to succeed in this challenging early stage of your new leadership role.

The Four Primary Tasks Explained

#1—*Understand the business mission of your team*

Understand your mission. Does this sound trite? After all, you have just been promoted to lead a team in customer support or marketing communications, or you are responsible for a product development initiative, so surely you know your mission. Let's pick on the new customer support supervisor who understands clearly that her job is to deliver outstanding support services and to raise customer support to a new level. What could be clearer than stepping in and making sure things are running smoothly and after awhile figuring out how to meet her manager's lofty expectations by raising the team's performance to levels previously unimagined in the world of customer support! Or is it so clear?

Outside of the comfortable little silo of support, the organization's strategy calls for a number of aggressive new programs to drive growth. During the next two years, the firm will be adding new domestic reseller channels, expanding into Europe and Asia and introducing new products designed to leapfrog competitors. One of the key requirements in the "go to market" plan for these initiatives is that support services be prepared to deal with challenges for increased volume, new time zones and complex new products that require the organization to gain new expertise. The situation is a lot more complicated than it first appeared! What should our now overwhelmed support supervisor do to get a good grasp on the true scope of her mission? First, she must ask a lot of questions of a lot of people on her team and across the organization to ensure that she fully understands her organization's strategies and her team's role in realizing those strategies. Second, she needs to understand the latitude that she is being given to make changes as well as the process for gaining buy-in and support for these changes. The ability to ask the right questions of the right people and then to listen carefully is an essential skill for any aspiring leader, and it is expected that you will have more questions than answers as you start your new role, so ask away—current team members, peers, managers, people in customer facing departments, customers if appropriate and especially the executives in your organization. Your direct manager and even his or her manager are great places to start.

Key questions to help understand your mission and the mission of your team

1. What is the organization's strategy and what are the key objectives to support strategy achievement?
2. What role does your group play in strategy execution?
3. How is this group/department/team to be measured against the strategy objectives and timetables?
4. What is the perception of how well this team is prepared today to execute on key objectives?

5. Am I taking over a team that has significant performance problems?

6. Am I responsible for leading a change-management initiative or are we just pursuing incremental changes in support of strategy execution?

7. How will I be evaluated as a manager?

8. What latitude do I have for driving change?

9. What is the process for proposing and gaining buy-in on the change?

10. What time constraints am I operating under?

While some of these topics may have been covered at a cursory level during the interview process, it is essential that you fully understand and have context for your company's situation and strategy, the state of your department, and the expectations that management has for you.

In addition to working vertically up the management food chain, it is essential that you understand how the world and your department look from other teams in the company. Talk with your internal customers or groups that serve your department, and as above, ask away. It is remarkable how much people will tell the new manager as a means of offering help, showing you how much they know, or attempting to exert influence. Regardless of their motives, listen carefully and learn.

Key cross-functional questions

1. In your experience working with my team, what works and what is broken?

2. What do you wish we would do better? Different?

3. Do we share a common view of the firm's strategy and a common view of our role(s) in supporting the strategy?

4. Do we have common processes and procedures to execute our tasks and to measure our performance and effectiveness?

5. Where are the bottlenecks in our processes and how can they be eliminated?

6. How do our combined activities affect other areas of the organization and their ability to serve our customers?

7. Do we have formal and regular communications between the teams to ensure that we are on the same page?

8. Are there opportunities to increase our shared objectives and collaboration as a means of improving performance?

9. Are your change-management initiatives likely to impact your needs for performance/deliverables/coordination with my group?

10. Are the goals, objectives and measures of each team transparent to each other?

As we mention repeatedly throughout this book, your effectiveness as a leader is a function of how well you understand the market forces impacting your business and how well you can tie those market forces to a firm's strategies and actions. Ultimately, the actions of your team need to be carefully integrated with those of the broader organization as part of the strategy execution plan. A great first step in building market-knowledge as a new leader is to invest time in talking and forming relationships with individuals in customer-facing groups. Although biased due to my sales and marketing background, these teams tend to have the best understanding of competitors, customers and issues supporting and challenging the business. Make certain that you meet early and often with representatives of groups close to the customer as a means of learning about and reinforcing your understanding of the marketplace.

Questions for market-facing teams

1. What are key factors supporting our growth?

2. What are key factors restricting our growth?

3. Is anything going on in the marketplace suggesting that we change?

4. What do we know about competitor strategies?

5. What are our customers telling us we need to do better/different?

6. What new customers groups are we chasing? Why?

7. What are our prospects telling us we need to do to win their business?

8. Are there new or disruptive products/services/technologies that are or will impact our business?

9. Why do we believe we will be successful with our new strategy?

10. How do you see my area changing/improving to support the strategy?
11. What are the most important things that the company needs to do to win in the market?

Finally, if you are working in a customer-facing group or can gain access to customers by working through your other associates, take advantage of the opportunity to visit, listen and learn.

Customer-focused questions

1. How do you use our products?
2. How do our products affect your business?
3. What do we do really well to support your business?
4. What do we need to improve to better support your business?
5. Please take me through a day in the life of someone that uses our products.
6. How do you view our products and services versus those of our competitors?
7. What are the primary challenges for your company/ department/ function?
8. Do you foresee an increased or decreased need for our products?
9. What do you hear in the industry about our company/ products?

I could continue to add to these lists indefinitely, hopefully you have gained some useful suggestions for asking questions that include issues that are far-reaching, market facing as well as introspective. Your ability to ask the right kinds of questions of your team, your managers, your co-workers and your customers is an indication of your maturity as a professional and as a leader. Your incessant questioning should begin on day one of your new role and continue throughout your career! Ultimately, your team will thank you for it as you are able to synthesize this information into thoughtful and compelling explanations and a call-to-action for their involvement, and your manager will thank you for your approach to generating great results! As a take away on communicating effectively, remember the 2:1 ratio: You have two ears and one mouth; use them in direct proportion and you will be well served!

The Four Primary Tasks Explained

#2—Get to Know Your Team and Let Them Get to Know You

Earlier in my career, I worked for a remarkable and hard-driving manufacturing executive with some great, commonsense approaches to leadership and management. One of those approaches that impressed me and has stuck with me to this day was his insistence that his manufacturing executives know the name of everyone on the factory floor—without the help of nametags stitched on their uniforms! He practiced what he preached, and upon visiting a facility—whether it was in the U.K. or U.S., would tour the factory and introduce himself to every worker. He would say that he, "wanted to know what they knew," and he would pick their brains for ideas and opportunities. On subsequent trips to the factory, he would greet these people by name and stop and chat about their ideas and how they were progressing on implementing the changes. It wasn't long before it seemed that he really did know everyone on the floor and impressively, he knew what they wanted to do to improve their function.

The energy that was generated by his visits was palpable. You could see it on their faces and hear it in their words that this head of a group of companies was someone that cared about their ideas and was someone good to work for. Of course, he was also using these visits to gauge the effectiveness of the general manager of the facility. One indicator was how well the general manager knew his people and their issues and ideas. On one occasion and after several warnings, he fired a general manager for failing to establish a relationship with the people doing the work.

Surprisingly, and for reasons that I have never understood, many new as well as experienced managers do a lousy job of meeting, much less getting to know their associates. Nothing is more important (after understanding your mission) than providing quality time to your associates in both group and one-on-one settings. Your willingness to meet with your team and to invest your time in listening to their ideas, issues and concerns is an important tool for building your leadership credibility. The perception that "you care" is powerful and priceless.

Establishing and maintaining an effective communications program is core to a leader's role. In the first few days and weeks of a new leader's tenure, the communication should be more about getting to know each other than about formal operations reports. Over time, you will need to establish the forums necessary to report on the business, to review performance and to problem-solve and brainstorm, but on day one, your primary issue is about "breaking the ice" with your new team.

Three Ice-Breaking Ideas for the New Leader

1. Set up an initial meeting with your team and ask everyone to make an introduction and describe what they do for the company and the department. Keep the business discussion light for this first meeting and ask some casual questions about the team's view of the marketplace, competitors and customer needs and issues. Commit to regular group sessions as a means of beginning your communications program and indicate when you will be scheduling the first business meeting. Also, communicate that you will be meeting with everyone individually over the next week or two and indicate the procedure for setting up the schedule. During this session, ask questions, listen more than you talk and take notes.

2. Live up to your commitment to schedule and conduct a one-on-one discussion with everyone during your first few weeks! Establish your list of questions regarding the business, people's professional objectives, their professional background and their ideas on what's working and what can be improved. Pass out these questions ahead of time so that everyone understands the meeting agenda. Again, listen more than you talk and take notes!

3. Following the conclusion of your group and individual meetings, set up your first business meeting, and make certain that you present a lessons-learned module as a result of your one on one sessions. Ask the team for feedback on whether they agree with your summary of the key issues and opportunities and challenge the group to help you prioritize an early to-do list.

Your up-front investment in time and your attention to the opinions of your people will create a positive buzz about your leadership style. You can sustain and extend this positive atmosphere by ensuring that your attention to people and commitment to communicating continues beyond the start-up phase and becomes part of the operating culture of the team. Your style for communicating with, listening to and building your understanding of your people will set you apart from just about every other manager you will come across during your career!

The Four Primary Tasks Explained

#3—Begin to Build Your Leadership Credibility

This topic is so important to your success as a leader that we expand upon it in a later chapter. However, understanding from day one, minute one, that you are only as effective as you are credible is critical to your success, so I am suggesting a number of "Quick Starts" to help you begin the process of building your leadership credibility. What makes this difficult is that building credibility is not so much a discrete task on your to-do list, but something that occurs over time and based on many interactions and observations. Your credibility is a measure of your worth as a leader, so pay close attention and remember that every interaction is an opportunity to add or subtract from your personal credibility bank account.

Credibility Quick-Start #1: Attitude is Everything!

As a leader, the moment you walk in the door on day one and forever more, you will be judged on everything that you say and do. Like a celebrity in the public spotlight, every word and action will be observed, interpreted and often replayed out of context. You need to constantly remember that everything that you say and do says something about you, your intentions and your attitude. Learning to watch what you say as well as how you say it is an important lesson that many leaders learn the hard way. In chapter seven, we will describe how to leverage this situation by adding drama into your leadership style.

You need to consistently portray a positive, reinforcing, empathetic, can-do attitude, even in the face of problems or disaster. Your quiet confidence in the face of a challenge will infect your team and ensure that people focus on problem solving instead of panicking, Alternatively, an irreverent attitude towards a senior executive or a depressed attitude in the face of adversity will carry negative messages to your team. Your mother's advice of "if you don't have something good to say, then don't say it," should resonate in your mind when you are tempted to show your frustration with others, with the company or with your own situation. Keep your attitude positive, empathetic and respectful as a means of building your ideal leadership persona and as a means of strengthening your credibility.

Credibility Quick Start #2: Energy supports attitude!

Your energy like your attitude is infectious. Teams and companies run on energy, and it is your job to understand how to dial this up when it is needed. If you have ever worked in an organization that is growing, developing new products and excited about the future, you can sense the energy in people's actions and conversations. Alternatively, in an organization that is struggling, the energy level is often depressed, exacerbating an already difficult situation. What many leaders don't grasp is that the energy of a team can be managed, and it is the leader's job to learn how to dial it up or tone it down depending upon circumstances.

At start-up, the best thing that you can do to affect group energy is to make certain that yours is visibly high—without being obnoxious. Over time, you will learn to manage the energy level of the team as a way to drive performance. However, on day one there is only one button to push on the energy panel—your own.

Don't discount the power of your enthusiasm and volume to let everyone know that you are glad to be in the new role and excited to help the team tackle the challenges in front of them. Reinforce your excitement and energy with frequent interactions. Ask questions, listen and learn from your teammates. Over time, engage them in active problem solving and updating and keep pushing politely for forward progress with their activities. Highlight the successes and lead the constructive debrief over failures. But most importantly, remember that on day one and day one thousand, your energy level sets the base line for the energy level of your team. If you are naturally more introverted than extroverted, you will need to learn how to turn it up in this situation, and if you are naturally extroverted, well just be careful to not be too obnoxious! Remember, energy supports attitude—keep it dialed up.

The Four Primary Tasks Explained

#4—Understand What Everyone is Doing and Why

Similar to the manufacturing executive referenced earlier in the chapter, I really want and need to understand what my people know, what they are doing and what they are thinking about their priorities. In general, most people conscientiously pursue their tasks and even work on optimizing what it is that they do. This of course completely discounts whether what they are doing is the right in the first place. Later in the book, we will examine the subtle importance and difference between "doing the right things," and "doing things right." It is remarkable how much opportunity cost is incurred by individuals and teams blindly pursuing and even perfecting tasks that are fundamentally immaterial to the firm's success. This "Manager's Dilemma," is often seen in the creation and routing of operations reports which are dutifully constructed and proudly distributed like clockwork and then summarily ignored by most or all recipients. You can set your watch by the distribution of that report—it just doesn't matter to anyone. You will want to identify these pockets of irrelevant perfection early in the process, as you will need this precious bandwidth later as you seek to align your limited resources around the real priorities of the business.

With every intention of being redundant, one of your key objectives is to reconcile the tasks that your team executes today with those that need to be executed to help achieve key strategy objectives. You need to understand what people are doing and why they think it is important. Because people rankle at having their reason for existence called into question, you need to not only ask the right questions but also ask them in the right way. Manage this process properly and you reinforce the perception that you are interested in what people are doing, that you value their input and you are focused on learning about the business. Do it wrong and it will seem to everyone like an uncomfortable medical examination.

Suggestions for understanding what your team is doing

1. People love to talk about what they do and what they've done to make it better. Solicit information on their tasks in a non-invasive, non-threatening manner versus a cross-examination style. Set up a follow-on meeting (your second one-on-one) and ask people to present what it is they do and how they believe that their output is leveraged by the organization. Let them know that this is a great time to offer suggestions or improvement ideas that they "wish they could implement," and that you are interested in those ideas. This is not disingenuous…you really should be interested.

2. Introduce a simple ranking system where individuals can prioritize their activities from order of perceived most important to the firm to least. I like to use an "A, B, C" system versus numbering, where A's are the most important and C's the least important. The forced ranking allows no more than 3 A's, with everything else a B or C.

3. During your group meetings, let the participants attempt to reach consensus on what their key tasks/deliverables are, and to force rank them. Assign someone from the group to facilitate this discussion and you simply ask clarifying questions.

4. Instead of asking about what people are doing, challenge individuals and teams to identify those things that they should potentially not be doing and again seek a ranking. The list of things that we shouldn't do may include tasks that are out of date and no longer significant, or things that potentially would be better off with another group. (Just beware of this last one, as the list of things that people perceive should be handled by other groups will pile up fast.)

5. If the team already has regular business meetings to review project activities, milestone achievement and progress, sit in on those sessions. You need to resist the urge to cancel those sessions and assert your own meeting schedule and format, as this knee-jerk tactic communicates your mistrust of the prior operations of the group. Instead, use these operations meetings as valuable learning opportunities. A keen observer will develop an understanding of group dynamics, individual capabilities, operational effectiveness and efficiency of the team and of course, you will learn what people are doing.

Consider the five tips above as valuable tools in helping you develop your leadership style. Ultimately, you will be in charge of defining roles, establishing priorities and creating the operating mechanisms for your team. However, at start-up, you are responsible for your own education—for developing a clear understanding of what is being done and not being done, and for how people view their roles and priorities. Your ability to get people talking in comfortable and professional settings will determine how people open up to you and how quick they begin to develop trust in you. Like so many tasks outlined in this book, your primary role is to shut up and listen. You will have ample opportunity to be heard as time progresses.

Six Agenda Killers and How to Avoid Them

The number of possible distractions to your primary agenda is some multiple of the number of items on the agenda. On occasion, you will realize your day is over and you will wonder what you did to make forward progress on the important issues, and why you allowed yourself to be so easily distracted. Take solace in the fact that you are not alone in the battle to make forward progress and use your end of day frustration to galvanize you and allow you to refocus on the real issues of your start-up role. As one executive commented during the research phase of this book, it is important for leaders to, "not focus on the details, but to detail the focus." I interpret this clever turn of words to mean that the leader needs to continuously make adjustments to ensure that the focus is on the material issues and off of the urgent-unimportant. A number of the more insidious agenda killers include:

1. *Volunteering for or agreeing to sit on every committee that you are invited to join.*

   As a new leader, your popularity will grow to a point where the opportunities for you to participate in will grossly exceed your available time. Learn to say "no," nicely, while choosing the one or two activities that will help you network across your organization and provide you with some measure of visibility.

1. *Spending too much time trying to become friends with your team.*

   Many early career leaders place too much emphasis on becoming "one of the gang," jeopardizing their credibility establishment with their team-members and potentially creating situations that will cloud their judgment on the tough issues ahead. Pace yourself on the relationship development, and focus on the business priorities at hand. There will be ample opportunity to forge friendships over time, especially after you have established your leadership credibility.

3. *Getting bogged down in historical data*

   You should resist the temptation to become hypnotized or paralyzed with the data for your area of operation, especially when you have no context for the information. Instead, focus on the questions outlined earlier and listen carefully. As you begin to understand the business and issues, the data and reports will become meaningful.

4. *Ignoring the subtle resistance of your team members.*

   All new leaders face some sort of subtle resistance at some point during their start-up process. You would be naive to think that on day one of your new role, everyone is ready to line up behind you and start marching. Ultimately, the cure for subtle resistance is a combination of time, familiarity and the team's belief in you as a credible, competent and caring leader. Your focus on the four primary tasks as well as paying careful attention to the lessons on building credibility covered in this book, will serve you well.

5. *Not being sensitive to pace.*

   This one is ripe for a good sports analogy. If you are a marathon runner, you adjust your pace to take into account your own capabilities as well as the perceived strategies of your competitors. As a leader, you are setting the pace for a group of runners, and it is easier to get it wrong than to get it right. Move too quickly with change and you risk confusing and exhausting your team. Move too slowly, and people become bored as the world seems to pass them by. Leverage the processes outlined above for getting to know your team and for developing an understanding of their activities, priorities and inner-workings. Your application of the right processes and your focus on building credibility will help establish an effective pace for you and the team.

6. *Assuming that you alone own the agenda*

   "Agenda Tug of War" is something that new managers often play with their teams. Many first-time managers are quick to outline their magnificent and compelling agenda for team improvement and conquering of the known world before they have established the proper credibility and sought the guidance of their team members. The team rankles at having the new manager force their agenda upon them, and will resist subtly and not so subtly.

   Your ability to help your team identify their major change initiatives and suggest approaches for achieving those changes is fundamental to your success. Your ability to create the environment where these ideas and approaches are drawn out, adopted and acted upon will in large part determine your success as a leader. While you have the right and responsibility to ensure that the focus stays on the right things, it should be your objective to get the broader team engaged in defining the priorities and agenda in support of achieving the firm's strategy. When your agenda becomes their agenda, the tug of war is over and you've all won.

Thoughts from Rich: Promoted From Within or "What Did I Do to Deserve This?"

Here we find a glaring paradox in organizational life. This is the most common promotion scenario for new leaders, but the least well managed. Significant time is dedicated to training new leaders on administrivia like completing forms, but virtually no time and attention is given to recognizing and dealing with the possible land mines associated with a move from team member to team leader. Makes you wonder how these new leaders succeed given the potential for disaster associated with these moves.

Promoting from within is a good thing for organizations. Research abounds to support a preference for developing and promoting internal leaders versus looking outside the firm for them. The direct benefits include the increased likelihood of success in the new role due to working with a known entity, reduced expense to fill the position, shorter ramp up time and increased likelihood of retention. With this in mind it is even more curious as to why organizations aren't universally committed – or perhaps we should say 'invested' - in the care and handling of leaders who are promoted from within the team.

Key challenges that <u>all</u> leaders need to be prepared for are covered throughout this book, but we felt the unique circumstances of being promoted from within a team merit special consideration. If you are about to make a move like this, or have recently moved up from inside – or even if you are a manager promoting a first time leader from within the ranks – please read on. You will find valuable insights that will help avoid some key rookie mistakes. As the old saying goes, you only get one chance to make a good first impression.

Special Considerations For Internally-placed First Time Leaders

- *Try to be yourself as much as possible. Granted you have a new role and there are different expectations for you, but if you begin to act differently your team will know and you will start making debits from whatever credibility you have established to date. Remember, your teammates have seen you in action for some period of time. You should trust in yourself and your instincts to carry on in largely the same manner as you did before. You no doubt demonstrated leadership traits in the past, which were precursors to being promoted.*

- *Act like a leader all the time. In meetings, in the lunchroom, at home. If you believe that leadership is more about who you are as a person than it is about your day job, over time this behavior will become second nature.*

- *Think of yourself as still being part of the team. Sort of. Your recent promotion aside, you are no better or worse than your team members, or more or less valuable, but you do have a different role. All parties should recognize that your role is different from theirs, but is still an integral function for achieving success together. You can't be successful without them and vice versa.*

CONGRATULATIONS, YOU HAVE A TEAM! NOW WHAT?

- *Share your view of your role with the team as a way to reinforce that your circumstances have changed. This includes tasks, duties, responsibilities, time constraints, etc. Include your new boss's expectations as well. Make it clear that the purpose of your role is primarily about the team's results and the firm's strategy objectives, not necessarily your own personal work.*

- *Seek feedback from the team on your promotion and any concerns or issues they may have. Your objective here is to get these things in the open so they can be addressed as needed. You can expect that one meaningful concern is losing somebody they felt was a friend and perhaps an ally and in return gained a new boss. Your skill in eliciting the dialog and dealing with concerns in an open, frank, and candid manner will develop with time and repetition, but this is a place to start.*

- *Be on the lookout for the skeletons. You know where they are hidden, and you can't vanquish all of them on your first day or week or month, but don't let them scare you! The expression, "call 'em as you see 'em," in this scenario means that you should deal with issues as they come up. Suggesting to a former peer that you are, "keeping an eye on them," for something you had seen in the past is not a recommended course of action. When you see the behavior you are concerned about deal with it promptly at the time. Don't reference past occurrences, just address the incidents that occur on your watch, and confirm your expectations going forward*

- *Resist the temptation to mold your former team members into your clone even if you were an outstanding team member. There are two very important lessons here. First, imposing your personal values on others is a path to disaster. One of the best ways to build resistance in team members is to force things on them, particularly your style and work habits. Second, you need to demonstrate appreciation for the diversity within your team in such a way that encourages new or different ways of thinking to the table. Diversity, properly managed, can result in more vigor in problem solving, more robust exchanges during brainstorming sessions and a sense of inclusion that will cement your team members to each other and their mission.*

- *Don't try to change everything at once. There will be enough for the group to get used to with a new leader in place that you don't want to force them to change all their routines or processes as well. Show that you have considered things before you make a change versus creating the impression that the change is just for the sake of change or because you can. As we will expound on in another chapter, your operational focus should revolve around alignment with corporate objectives, and that needs to be apparent to your team. Knee-jerk changes can create the impression that it is YOUR agenda versus the firm's. Follow Art's advice in this chapter for identifying and implementing change and you will do fine.*

A Word About the Selection Process

If you are in an organization that posts open positions, and you assume that some of your peers – which could include others on the same team or people on other teams, in other departments, etc. – are also expressing interest in a leadership opening, don't feel your interest needs to be a secret. As a potential leader you should have the confidence to openly express your interest in a leadership role, and the maturity to handle that disclosure with a genuine degree of humility. Nobody likes a braggart. Conducting your self appropriately is a precursor to serious consideration for leadership positions. For example – are you willing to demonstrate genuine support and encouragement for others who are competing for the same position? After all, at least one of you will be disappointed when the process is completed.

A Special Note for Managers Who Make Promotion Decisions

First time leaders who take over their old team deserve extra attention on your part. If the team operates in a mature fashion this will be less of an issue for you. Either way, you can't assume the group will self regulate and come back to center right after a new leader is installed, so stay close. The new leader will benefit from your involvement and the team will benefit from the results of that involvement.

Staff members at all levels will be more supportive of the organization as a whole if they can feel proud of the decisions that are made. This is a factor whether the promotion is for a leadership role or a more advanced individual contributor role. If the organization makes a bad decision the troops will be aware of it – probably before management – and promoting from within will be seen as a joke or a patronage benefit bestowed for reasons other than merit. Keep this in mind when you are in a position to make promotion decisions.

Finally, don't expect to make everybody happy every time with the results, and seek guidance from your HR representative on what you can or cannot disclose about the selection process. As a rule of thumb, I discourage open discussion with the team about why candidates weren't selected, but I encourage that dialogue about the successful candidate. Sharing your point of view with the team will help them understand the selection criteria, your expectations of the role and your assessment of the individual you selected. It's a great way to set the table – keeping the lines of communication open, even on thorny topics, and an opportunity to demonstrate your support for the new boss.

-Rich

Epilogue

Your goal is to end up right where I started this chapter—with the confidence, attitude and know-how to assume responsibility for a team and do the right things to quickly and to effectively align the team around the organization's strategy. You want to get the focus off of personal anxieties and on to the pursuit of business objectives. The elevation of a new team leader creates a sense of anxiety and discomfort for most or all team participants. Your recognition of these most human of qualities is important to your ability to understand what makes people and teams tick, as well as to your ability to establish yourself as a good communicator and ultimately an interested and engaged leader. While it may sound manipulative it's not intended that way. An effective leader is able to command strong loyalty by banishing fears and personal concerns in favor of creating value for the business. Remember, you are in the business of managing human beings. You signed on for this, so be a great student and a greater practitioner. By the way, I've often thought that business would be easy if it were not for the people. Of course, people are all that we have.

Discussion Questions-Susan's First Day

- *What can Susan do to grab control of the situation?*
- *After reviewing this chapter, how would you reshape Susan's sixty day 'to do' list?*
- *What would a personal communications plan for Susan look like?*

For ideas on how the authors view the situation at Apex and the issues outlined above, visit the Leadership Resource Center at www.management-innovations. com, and click on Practical Lessons-Discussion Questions.

PART THREE
SUCCEEDING ALL OF THE TIME

PREFACE TO CHAPTER 6

THE ASSASSIN AND THE BIG TALKER

A well-placed comment...

Alan Michaels, Sales Director for Vertical Markets at Apex, stared at the chart showing his team's year to date performance. Actual results were significantly behind targets, and Alan knew that this could be trouble for him. His counterpart, Sharon Franklin, who runs field sales, was having just the opposite kind of year. Sharon's teams were knocking it out of the park, and Alan suspected that this meant she was likely to have the inside track for senior director.

Alan was aware that Sharon was going through some tough times at home that impacted her ability to be as active in the field and with customers as she should have been. Her managers were pitching in to cover some regional meetings while she took care of the situation on the home front. Alan had heard this directly from one of Sharon's managers who indicated that he was happy to help her out after all she had done for him in his career.

Alan knew that their respective boss, Fred, was a stickler for time in the field. He wondered how Fred would react if he knew that Sharon's managers were covering for her. Later that afternoon as Alan was wrapping up a pipeline review with Fred, his casual comment about hoping Sharon was doing ok with her personal issues, seemed to catch Fred off guard.

10,000 words creates a picture...

Jeff Jones was in a zone. He had been preaching to his team for 20 minutes about the need to pick up productivity and cut costs. He knew he was good in front of a group, but he suspected that this was one of his best performances. He had worked in everything but the kitchen sink for this one. Belt tightening, work smarter and harder, innovate, do more with less, and anything else he could think of that would motivate his team. And he saved the best for last... possible job cuts at the end of the year if things didn't pick up. He knew he had the group where he wanted them when most were just staring at their notepads with dour looks on their faces. "They've got the message by now," he thought with a feeling of satisfaction.

CHAPTER 6
GROWING YOUR PERSONAL CREDIBILITY ACCOUNT

Your credibility is your currency as a leader, and like most currencies that the authors have had experience with, it is slow to accumulate and quick to dissipate. A credible leader is one that has earned the trust and confidence of her associates by treating people with respect, ensuring that her words and actions match and leading according to the principles suggested in *The Nine Attributes of Great Leaders*. The credible leader is a leader that leaves a lasting positive impression on the careers and the lives of her associates, often inspiring people to attempt and achieve more than they ever thought possible.

Inherent in the attribute of credibility is the formula for success as a leader. Importantly, this formula is not hidden away in a vault like the formula for Coca Cola. Rather, it is on display for everyone to see and to use in their work environment. It is simple. Treat people with respect, ensure that your actions match your words and remember that your job is to motivate and inspire. Why so many leaders choose to ignore the formula and pursue success by force or manipulation and without the credibility that would make their lives so much easier is difficult to understand.

During the research phase for this book, we asked people what it was about leaders that they admired that made them credible. Almost universally, the answers included comments about actions matching words, treating people with respect and the ability to articulate a compelling vision for the future. Surprisingly however, most of the discussions started out positive and quickly turned towards the attributes of leaders that destroyed their credibility and ultimately, their effectiveness. The laundry list of credibility killers included some truly odious traits and habits:

- Lack of follow-through
- Insincerity
- Deceitfulness
- Maintaining hidden agendas
- A personal agenda versus a company focus
- Dishonesty, self-serving behavior
- Taking credit versus dispensing credit
- Not going to bat for you or the team
- Inability to get to know team members on a personal basis
- A style of communication that does not convey respect

The animated discussions and priceless quotes about the traits of bad leaders, including my favorite, "When the say doesn't match the do, the fish rots from the head," were telling. The interviewees in this study indicated in unambiguous terms that they preferred to work for someone they deem credible, especially if they felt challenged and respected as people and professionals. The results match with my own long-held belief that we truly seek to work for someone we believe in, and the basis of this belief is our perception that they are credible individuals.

It is challenging for me to write this chapter without feeling like I am preaching to you, and perhaps I am. Your personal credibility is so important to your success as a leader, that for me to do anything less than drum this into you would be grounds for malpractice. If you remember cringing as a child when your parents reminded you to be honest, respect your elders, use good table manners and wear clean underwear at all times, this chapter on building credibility might seem reminiscent. Nonetheless, if you are like most people, the words to live by that we learned in our youth have proven golden as adults. I sincerely hope this lesson on credibility will add to your store of gold.

Your Personal Credibility Bank Account

Your elevation to a leadership role has changed your lot in life. The skills that worked so well for you as a soloist or individual contributor are not the same skills that you will draw upon and develop as a leader of people. Your new mission is to gain the trust and confidence of people below, next to and above you in an effort to push an agenda of programs, objectives and ultimately achievements that support your firm's strategies. If you want people to believe in you and to listen to your ideas as well as to seek you out as a sounding board for their ideas, you must be credible. People must believe that you are genuine, honest, capable and in earnest about your willingness to listen, act, experiment and even learn from your mistakes.

Your personal credibility cannot be measured, nor can it be purchased. Credibility is like an intangible bank account. From the moment someone meets you, they develop their own perception of who you are and what you are all about. Based on repeated exposures to you, they either debit or credit your credibility account. The deposits are hard earned and the withdrawals fast, frivolous and unseen. It is easy to go negative with your balance and once there, nearly impossible to turn things around. Whether you know it or not, your words, your actions and your approaches are measured and judged and your credibility account affected accordingly. This is one situation where deficit spending is fatal to your leadership future.

Warning—Your Title does not Confer Lasting Credibility

Many otherwise competent people miss this one. Your promotion provides what I describe as momentary-benefit-of-the-doubt credibility. For a split second, people will assume that because someone thought well enough of you to put you into this role, that you are capable. However, the decay rate of this credibility is remarkably fast, often dissipating as soon as you open your mouth. Don't get caught up in your new self-importance and think that anyone around you is buying off on your "I'm in charge" shtick. Title does not confer lasting credibility.

The Really Bad Habits of Ineffective Leaders

We were reminded during our research that one of the most powerful ways to learn how to do things right is by observing people doing things wrong. The interviewees were adamant that they learned some of their best leadership lessons by serving under someone that they deemed a poor leader. Rather than preach at you for the next ten pages, we decided to poke some fun at some of the bad habits of ineffective leaders as a means of reinforcing how not to lead. Of course, for anyone of our former associates, managers or for the publisher's lawyers, please rest easily as these examples are an amalgam of habits and styles, and any resemblance to any person, living or dead, is purely coincidental. Now that the disclaimer is out of the way, it time to move on to some really bad examples and see how otherwise intelligent people manage to shoot themselves in the leadership foot!

The "Too-Busy" Boss

We all know this character. This is the boss that dodges and ducks one on one time and tough issues, always promising to get back to you, but never quite finding the time or opportunity. As you approach their office, a look of panic crosses their face and they immediately reach for their phone, their keyboard or any other device that might rescue them from unwanted face time. Corner this leader after a meeting to raise an important issue, and you are often rewarded with a tap dance that would make Fred Astaire jealous as the leader attempts to work his way out of the corner and move towards a safe location as far away from the needy co-worker as possible. A great example of the "Too-Busy" creature was the executive that when faced with a compelling issue, would invariably respond with, "That's an important topic and we should talk about it at the right time." Unfortunately for this executive's team members, it was never the right time.

Consistently being too busy to pay attention to your people and to understand and address the tough issues of the day is an outstanding way for leaders to destroy their credibility. Not paying attention to people is an overt form of disrespect. The leader, through his actions, is indicating that the issues and ideas of staff members are not important. The staff members quickly become frustrated with lack of substantive discussion and the likely lack of timely decision making. Overall, this approach is guaranteed to reduce morale, impede progress and frustrate everyone in its wake.

The All Talk, No Action Leader

This character is a near cousin of the "Too-Busy" leader, and while some members of this group are easily recognized, others only show their true selves over time. The more elusive form is usually polished and articulate, offering grand pronouncements in public, and regaling you with descriptions of past conquests in private. They never focus on your issues, and while they might provide you with face time, you can forget about quality-time. Finally, when push comes to shove and you are looking for this manager to support your cause, you will have to look for him on the back of a milk carton, because he will be conveniently missing! Big talkers that keep on talking without taking action suffer from rapidly shrinking credibility accounts.

The Chameleon Manager

A close relative of several of these leaders, the Chameleon is constantly testing the water to determine whom she should align with, which is code for figuring out who might be able to help her the most with that next promotion. The speed at which this manager changes opinions is unrivaled in the animal kingdom, and you learn quickly that if your issue does not fit with what the Chameleon believes is in her best interests, your idea is guaranteed to end up as road kill. It only takes one or two examples of this behavior for the credibility account of the Chameleon to drain to zero.

The Never- Make-A-Decision Leader

Often friendly and engaging on the outside, the Never-Make-A-Decision leader secretly fears making a decision for which they might be held accountable, or which might require them to actually do some work. To him, the lesser evil is to avoid decisions at all costs, and then when things go wrong, he covers his rear by lamenting the unapproved actions of others. A side benefit is that he does not get bogged down in too much work, and remains free to socialize and act leader-like, without really doing too much. Frequent symptoms of this leadership style include widespread demoralization, rampant frustration and generally lousy results. This leader's credibility account is bankrupt.

The Game-Playing, Fork-Tongued Boss

This leader operates by keeping people off balance. Prone to playing people off against each other, he enjoys telling you what you want to hear and regales in telling you things he should not tell you about your peers. Of course, he does the same to you behind your back. The Game-Playing, Fork-Tongued variety is difficult to spot, but once their cover is blown, their credibility account is over-drawn and quickly closed.

The "At My Last Company, We Did It This Way" Leader

These intrepid leaders would have you believe that they have a leg-up on everyone else, because they clearly spent most of their career in an organization that the rest of us mere mortals can only dream about. While non-toxic, this person is a bore that sucks the energy and innovation out of any problem-solving situation with his constant references to the utopian state that existed at his last company, where everything went right and everyone was a genius. More often than not, this legendary, do-no-wrong company has ceased to exist, and employees of this manager find themselves wishing for ruby slippers that would send him home.

The Micro-Manager

She is the most common type of dysfunctional leader, constantly showcasing her intense distrust of anyone by looking over shoulders and suggesting how people do their jobs. She quickly suffocates her team with her unceasing involvement in everyone's business, and is always surprised when the team members race for the door in pursuit of positions anywhere but with her.

The Public Humiliator

Clearly operating with an inferiority complex about something, the Public Humiliator feels compelled to let everyone know that he is in charge by mercilessly drubbing associates with an audience present. He enjoys showcasing his power in public and naively believes that it makes him look important. You will recognize the team members of this type of a leader by the way they cower in front of him, and do everything possible to avoid his attention in a group setting. The Humiliator's credibility account is always negative.

The Everyone's Best Buddy After Work Manager

This leader uses a bait and switch approach to leading, ruling with an iron fist during the day only to morph into everyone's best friend at the bar after work. After awhile, his quick-to grab-the-tab approach at the bar helps develop a loyal group of minions that do his bidding during the day. Ignore the social time at your own risk! While this leader has no credibility outside of his minions, it is difficult to survive and even more difficult to prosper unless you are one of the gang.

The Assassin

Beware this efficient killing machine. The Assassin is a combination of several of the above, choosing to aim his weapons at anyone that is perceived as threatening. He will work covertly to sabotage his enemy's efforts, and often succeeds. Assassins are generally respected as leaders and are careful to remain above suspicion while expertly executing a contract. This character is a striking example of the adage, "people reap what they sow." Eventually these leaders get caught, and when this day comes, there are very few tears shed over the assassin's demise.

Unfortunately, it is easy and just a little fun to describe the different styles of some truly bad leaders. Without a doubt, you will encounter all of the above and likely many other leaders that ply their trade in complete ignorance of what their true role is and what it takes to motivate and to inspire others to succeed. Rather than building and creating, their objectives include control over people, assertion of power to feed their egos and internal turf building as a means of enhancing their careers. In the interest of growing their careers and leading the way they believe they need to lead to get ahead, they are actually 180 degrees wrong. Every competent leader understands that you gain more influence by distributing power and authority, yet these leaders choose to do the opposite. And while their abuse of their power may allow them to play their games and gain compliance for short periods of time, they are completely non-credible and will not make the list of great leaders in anyone's mind. People will not move mountains for non-credible leaders.

How do you know when you've developed the bad habits of ineffective leaders?
During a review of this chapter, my co-author asked me the very appropriate question of how does someone know that they are starting to resemble one or several of those bad leaders outlined in the examples? Great question! In an organization with a mature 360-degree review system, the leader would likely learn about any aberrant leadership practices pretty quickly. In the absence of the review process, we encourage the leader to seek feedback from others, and listen carefully for what they mean, not just what they say. If you suffer from some bad leadership habits, it is likely that your associates may not want to confront you, and risk their own necks by punching you in the metaphorical nose, even if you ask. If you receive pat answers of, "everything's fine," or "no, you're great," then beware. Also, you can take some of the discomfort out of the discussion by asking the following types of non-threatening questions:

- How can I better support your efforts?
- How do you feel that we can improve our effectiveness in working together?

- What can I do to help you make your objectives for the next quarter?
- Are there things that I can do differently that would allow you to increase your contribution to the team?

And while an honest answer from a direct report will still take a small leap-of-faith on their part, your focus on helping them succeed and their carefully worded answers may give you some clues to where your approach is failing. Ultimately however, it is up to you to have the desire to be an effective leader as well as the emotional intelligence to recognize your faults when someone is honest enough to bring them to your attention.

Building Credibility is a Constant Work In Process

When it comes to leadership, your intentions count. Blind ambition might help you climb the ladder, but it won't help you galvanize groups of people to move mountains, conquer markets and develop a culture of sustained excellence. Step one on your journey towards becoming an effective or even great leader is to ensure that when people look and listen they find you believable, honest, empathetic, consistent, capable, and interested and every other adjective that sounds like it supports the Boy Scout motto. "A scout is trustworthy, loyal, helpful, friendly, courteous, kind, obedient, thrifty, brave, clean and reverent." Corny? Yes! Correct? Absolutely! Easy to live up to? Not a chance!

Credibility is a function of character and it is generally understood that a person's character is formed earlier in life than later. If your character predisposes you to the behaviors described in the prior section, there's not much we can do other than point out the evils of your way, and in fact, we would suggest you quit reading now and save yourself some time.

Thoughts from Rich: Another Perspective on Personal Change

Can people really change later in life? OK, let's assume we are talking fundamental change beyond getting more exercise or trying a different line of work. What about enduring personal traits like being an irascible bastard? Seriously. I have an example in mind, but let's start by setting context. Yes, research shows that much of an individual's behavior or personality, including the things we may ascribe as character, values, enduring personal traits, etc., are formed early in life. It's one of the things developmental psychologists such as Erik Erikson and Jean Piaget agree on. Bypassing the whole nature-nurture debate for now, we can probably agree that parents, teachers, coaches, clergy, and family mem-

bers had roles early in our lives in shaping who we are as adults. *Throw into this the general human tendency to protect the status quo and resist change - particularly for adults – and you can appreciate that it's a rare human leopard that changes his spots. Even more provocative, imagine if somebody else suggests the need to change…you can almost hear the heels digging in. After all, clichés like "you can't teach an old dog new tricks"' have some foundation in reality or they wouldn't survive.*

True change is not impossible, however. Like the old joke: how many psychologists does it take to change a light bulb? It only takes one but it takes a long time and the light has to want to change. Let me share one remarkable story about a strong inner drive to change – it's about the previously mentioned irascible bastard. He decided the direction of his life and career would benefit from several fundamental changes and he set out to recast himself in a variety of ways. Included in his goals for change were the following:

- *Managing his temper and openly soliciting feedback from peers and subordinates.*
- *Completing his undergraduate degree.*
- *Doing something about going bald at a relatively early age and the impact he felt it had on others' perception of him.*
- *Committing to running as a means of improving his fitness.*

How did he do with his pursuits? Extremely well. In fact, surprisingly well. These weren't small changes, and often people are most successful with a focus on one goal. Much like a manager's corrective process when a team member has more than one problem area, your manager or HR advisor will likely suggest that you select the most important item to focus on. That doesn't mean wholesale change is impossible. In this case, he was hugely committed to change which was reflected in is results. For example:

- *<u>Becoming a more nurturing manager and sensitive to the feelings of others.</u> He knew he was a demanding manager, but came to realize the impact his approach had on others and how it made them feel. It wasn't enough in this case that he routinely solicited feedback relative to the behaviors he wanted to modify, but he made demonstrable efforts to change. He extended his own personal development approach to the people who worked for him and really came to appreciate the bonds that resulted from committing to the development of others as much as he had committed to himself. He recast himself as a supportive manager people sought to work for rather than one to be avoided. Perhaps most importantly, he made these changes in his way of interacting with people without losing* *his demanding nature – he just pursued results in a more thoughtful, effective way.*

- *<u>Returning to school and receiving his bachelor's degree at the age of 50.</u> He is quick to credit others for encouraging him in this pursuit, but he was on his own when it required attending classes at night and studying on the weekends.*

- *<u>Joining the Hair Club for Men to resolve his concern about his balding appearance.</u> To his credit, he was very public about telling others about his choice, and while this may seem like small potatoes to others, it was obviously something that meant a great deal to his self-image. A very powerful thing, indeed, which probably contributed to the steely resolve he showed in the other areas of change.*

- *<u>Running the Chicago Marathon was a focal point of his commitment to running.</u> Not only did he lose weight and feel better, but he competed in the marathon the following year. His approach to a training regimen reflected his approach to these changes overall. I recall somebody asking him if he ran one morning because the weather was cold and rainy. He said he did, and further commented that he made a commitment to himself and to training, and that commitment didn't take days off because the weather was less than agreeable.*

His professional career moved ahead and beyond the organization where he felt he might have otherwise been stranded, and when I last talked with him he was a senior vice president in a large, well-known firm. The ultimate leadership economy! In fairness, there is no way to tell for sure how this story would have otherwise ended, but my prediction would have included an end to his career in management – he would either stay at his present level or be assigned the dreaded special projects role.

Let's come back to reality – in nearly 25 years of human resources work this is one remarkable case I can tell you about. It's not the only one. However, I could fill a book with the discussions I have had with people who give lip service to change but can't or won't commit to it. Why? Well, that's a different book.

-Rich

The Nine Credibility Builders
Rules for Effective Leaders to Live By

If your basic intent is to do good by yourself and for others, and you get the fact that leadership is a compelling and difficult calling, then this section will prove invaluable. *The Nine Credibility Builders-Rules for*

Effective Leaders to Live By, offers guidance and suggestions for establishing and strengthening your credibility to aid in your journey to become an effective leader. With one last reminder that credibility is earned not bestowed, and that it is a laborious and slow process, easily derailed by a slip up, let's learn the lessons that were taught the day the ineffective leaders skipped school.

1. **Your positive attitude and high energy level** are infectious to everyone around you! It's hard to be "on" all of the time, but you need to remember that people are feeding off your excitement and can-do approach. We talked about the importance of these characteristics as part of your start-up in Chapter 5, but they transcend start-up. If you are a successful leader, people will set their watch to your time and adapt their attitudes to your mood. Over time, your constant reinforcement of the right attitude and appropriate energy level begin to become part of the culture of a team. You will have many days when it takes effort to get there, but this is your obligation.

2. **Your approachability and a willingness to listen** even when it is inconvenient are powerful credibility builders. You will undoubtedly work for or around people that are chronically too busy to focus on the most important priorities, the needs and issues of their team members. Your understanding and reinforcement of your willingness to engage and deal with the issues that your direct reports face is a sign of respect, concern and commitment. This is not to say that you cannot establish ground-rules for efficient communications and in fact you should. A blanket open-door policy can be abused, while a semi-formal approach, a blend of scheduled and unscheduled contact, can work well for you.

     A practice of regular contact—either formal or informal is appropriate. I prefer to set the example by establishing an approach that fits with the needs, style and time constraints of my team member, versus something that is simply convenient for me. For example, a new front-line manager benefited from daily contact, so we found an almost daily early morning telephone call would tee up both of our days properly. He had the chance to update me on activities and issues, and I was committed to listening and perhaps offering suggestions. Another person, my top sales manager, benefited from tying off his day on the drive home by highlighting accomplishments and communicating next day challenges. In both cases, we all felt like we were updated and that we had ample opportunity to ask questions or make suggestions. Other associates might need only weekly contact, and you as manager need to develop a rhythm to the frequency and formality of your calls…often adapting to the individual's style. Scheduled group sessions are appropriate and important if executed properly, but I have always found frequent, informal opportunities to be the most effective. Of course, there will be times when someone needs you and it will be extraordinarily inconvenient for you. From time to time you will have to play the, "I am too busy at the moment," card, and that is fine, but you need to follow with a suggestion for a near-term slot that will be acceptable to the associate. If people abuse your accessibility, and some certainly will, you will need to address this separately. Meanwhile, remember that you show respect and concern when you take the time to do your job and engage with your team members.

3. **Your unimpeachable honesty** is unimpeachable. There are few absolutes in life, but this is one of them. Your integrity dictates your credibility, and honesty is fundamental to all of them. You should expect this of your charges as well. People have an uncanny ability to figure out when others cannot be trusted and when they are not always straight with the truth. You never want to have your honesty questioned, so do not do anything that calls it into question. One quick note on honesty versus stupidity. You will find yourself in many situations where you cannot answer a question due to non-disclosure or sensitivity issues. For example, if you are part of a merger or acquisition process you may be barred from talking about it or even acknowledging it to your associates. You cannot violate these trusts or fiduciary responsibilities and need to communicate the rather unsatisfying, "I cannot go into that," or some more eloquent derivative. You are being honest…while fulfilling on your privacy obligations. These can be painful situations where you feel as if your disclosure is required otherwise "people will talk," but there is no gray area. It might appear gray, but it is absolutely black or white.

4. **A visible agenda** is essential to strengthening your credibility. You need to be proactive in providing people context for what you are doing. Anything less creates an air of uncertainty and anxiety. For example, when leading a change management initia-

tive, I want everyone to understand what we are changing and why. I want them to understand the business drivers behind the change and at a high level what the process for change will be, including dealing with talent issues. It can be a difficult discussion and you might feel awkward being so open about initiatives that will affect the work lives of your associates, but anything less than full visibility is unacceptable. Managers that keep their agenda close to their vest are fooling themselves. People sense when "something is up," and your lack of communication regarding your intentions will quickly destroy their trust in you. Alternatively, as part of getting people on-board with new initiatives or significant change, communicating your intentions shows respect. This respect is paid in kind.

5. **Your commitment to doing the "right thing"** even if it is the difficult choice will pay credibility dividends beyond your imagination! Your job as teacher, role model and professional leader requires you to make the right choice at all times, even if it is painful. Whether it is holding up a shipment due to quality issues or scuttling a major initiative because it does not meet customer or corporate needs, you must choose correctly or risk destroying your integrity and credibility. Leading by example is a powerful teaching tool and is also a testament to your character. Again, there is nothing gray when it comes to doing the "right thing."

6. **Your minimal use of the personal pronoun, "I,"** says volumes about your character and enhances your credibility. Too many managers suffer from "I" diarrhea, to the point where they become laughing-stocks. Your job is to live up to that old coaching adage that says, "When we win, it's because of the team and when we lose, it's because of me." Your willingness to provide clear attribution and visibility to those responsible for victories will feed their basic need for recognition and will be readily observed and appreciated by all around you.

7. **Your interest and support of your associates professional development and interests** has a strange and powerful affect on people. They develop a deep and abiding respect for you and any reservations about your credibility melt away in their gratitude over the support that you provided. This most powerful of tools for you to create is one that is oft ignored by shortsighted managers focused on business objectives and day-to-day fire

fighting. If addressed at all, it is frequently filler for the annual review, lacking substance, an action plan and follow-through. Ultimately, it is your responsibility to align people and their talents with the right business objectives. Frequently, people find themselves in the wrong place or are interested in making a change in their professional lives. Your willingness to listen, understand and either identify initiatives or offer ideas and support for the interests will serve as a powerful proof point for your leadership style, integrity and credibility.

As an aside, I long ago decided that I would do everything within my power to encourage my associates to pursue advanced degrees, professional certifications or any form of additional education that would help them grow as people and professionals. This mission of mine had its roots in the shortsighted behavior of a manager who refused to provide me with the latitude to leave work thirty minutes earlier to commute to graduate school, in spite of my consistently outstanding reviews and my early arrival at work every day. I never understood this shortsighted concern for the time clock and most importantly, the lack of concern for my professional development. I transferred away from that manager, finished my degree and vowed to do the right thing for people the rest of my career.

8. **Your willingness to allow people to experiment and learn from their mistakes** speaks volumes about your self-confidence. The insecure manager will work to ensure that their charges do nothing that might cast the shadow of a mistake on their reputation. The self-confident manager will create a learning environment where people are encouraged to push the envelope in pursuit of business objectives. Victories and innovations are acknowledged and rewarded, and mistakes and failures are leveraged as powerful teaching tools. This approach creates a culture of innovation and often rewards the presiding manager with remarkable achievements.

9. **A profound sense of humility showcases your maturity and character** and builds remarkable amounts of trust, loyalty and credibility between you and your teammates. This should not be confused with subjugating your ego, but rather your humility ensures that your focus is on your team, the individuals and the business and their professional objectives. Most great leaders display tremendous egos. They love to win and losing drives

them crazy. Being outflanked by a competitor is a direct insult and if the loss was due to things that could have been controlled, you better stay out of their way. Nonetheless, win or lose, they understand that people drive the business, that people make up their customer base and that without these people they are and have nothing. Their ability to focus frustration on issues and turn a loss into a learning lesson, a new innovation and ultimately victory in the marketplace is a testament to their mature sense of humility. Self-discipline, self-confidence and a high emotional intelligence are pre-requisites for success in realizing this most important and visible of management and personality characteristics.

A summary of *The Nine Credibility Builders* is highlighted below as a quick reference. A printable document can be found in the Leadership Resource Center at www.management-innovations.com.

The Nine Credibility Builders
Rules for Effective Leaders to Live By

1. **Your positive attitude and high energy level are infectious to everyone around you.**
2. **Your attention to others and your willingness to listen are the ultimate signs of respect that you can pay your coworkers.**
3. **Honesty is not a some-of-the time policy.**
4. **A visible agenda builds trust. Broadcast yours constantly.**
5. **The only time to do "the right thing" is all of the time.**
6. **ABCDEFGH JKLMNOPQRSTUVWXYZ No I.**
7. **Your job is to support the career development of others. This is how you positively affect lives.**
8. **Mistakes are the best teachers...encourage them.**
9. **Humility is a virtue...practice it.**

Epilogue
We will end where we started—credibility counts. You will have ample opportunities to cut corners and simplify your day by ignoring your credibility quotient and taking the easy way out. You may be tempted to adopt some of the negative characteristics described earlier in the

chapter, and you may even rationalize that you are doing the right thing. Ignoring repeated calls for face-time with that high maintenance individual or playing politics to support your gain are at times tempting. You will make mistakes and you will say and do things that detract from the confidence and belief that people place in you. Your challenge is to minimize the mistakes and focus on leading with *The Nine Credibility Builders* clearly in mind every day. Eventually, doing the right thing all of the time becomes second nature, and this is where you can declare victory. In a closed environment like a department or a firm, lost credibility can never be regained. Your worth as a professional is at stake, so don't screw it up.

Discussion Questions: The Assassin and the Big Talker

- *Do you think that Victoria Pyott, Apex's CEO, would find the leadership styles of Alan and Jeff agreeable? Why or why not?*
- *If you were Fred, how would you deal with Alan's comment?*
- *How do you feel if you are a member of Jeff's team? Will his words inspire you to work harder and achieve more?*
- *How do you survive working for a boss like Jeff?*

For ideas on how the authors view the situation at Apex and the issues outlined above, visit the Leadership Resource Center at www.management-innovations. com, and click on Practical Lessons-Discussion Questions.

PREFACE TO CHAPTER 7

MARK'S MESS GETS MESSIER

Susan enjoyed the weekly lunch meetings with Mark. They were dealing with similar circumstances and they both agreed that it was helpful to share problems and ideas. Both were first time managers, and both had a strong commitment to Apex and to doing the best for their respective teams.

After a couple of rocky months, Susan felt like she was finally on the right track with her team, and she knew that she owed a large thanks to her manager, Pat, who had stayed involved enough to offer guidance and mentoring, but not too much to keep her from learning on her own.

Mark was a different case. "I feel like my team is in meltdown," lamented Mark. "I've had two resignations since I started in this role. I can't find and train people fast enough, and it seems like no one in the company wants to work in this department. To top it off, I just heard that sales is changing their structure again, but no one has bothered to tell me what they're doing or how it impacts us." he added. "Everyday, I run around like a crazy person, solving problem after problem, and by the time I show up the next morning, it starts all over again. I've never seen a group of people more reluctant to try and solve something on their own."

"Where's your manager in this picture?" asked Susan, thinking about all of the high level guidance she had received from Pat.

"Sam is a good guy," answered Mark, "but he's tied up in a lot of other things. He promised me when I took this job that he wouldn't be a micromanager, and so far, he's lived up to that promise."

CHAPTER 7
FORGET EVERYTHING ELSE, HERE'S YOUR REAL JOB—CREATING THE EFFECTIVE WORK ENVIRONMENT

You cannot see or touch your work environment, but you can most definitely observe it in the actions and behaviors of your team members. The environment determines how people interact, collaborate, problem-solve, brainstorm, innovate and overcome obstacles. The willingness of individuals or teams to take risks and the passion with which people pursue their jobs are all a function of the working environment that you as leader foster through your words and your actions. Ultimately, your success as a leader is dependent upon your understanding of this concept and your commitment to doing everything within your power to foster an effective work environment for your team.

If you are wondering why you have not had long talks with your manager about this part of your role, or why it is not spelled out in your job description, it is because most leaders do not recognize that this is the core of their job. They focus on managing tasks and schedules, and fail to recognize the power that they have to form the work environment and the impact that an effective environment has on productivity and performance. The problem starts with the job description.

The Problem with Most Job Descriptions

Your job description, if you have one, likely includes a myriad of responsibilities pertaining to the management of your functional area and associates, including hiring, firing, promoting, adhering to budgets and meeting performance targets. There may even be words that loosely describe your responsibility for developing and maintaining a professional and productive work environment. However, most job descriptions are formulaic lists of every task the up-line manager can fit on the form. My favorite is the ubiquitous, "And all other responsibilities as assigned." While a generic job description may be slightly better than no job description, it fails to truly describe the essence of your role as a leader. What is needed is a mission or charter for the leader (new or established) to serve as a guiding philosophy for their true role, and a constant reminder of how they should be spending their time. That is why I created *The Leader's Charter.*

Your Real Job Description—The Leader's Charter

I developed *The Leader's Charter* earlier in my career as a tool to keep me focused on my core mission as a manager, and then refined it over time to aid in the development of new leaders under my direction. While it has clearly evolved into a run-on sentence that will have grammarians reaching for their red pens, it has been my experience that it is a powerful teaching tool for aspiring and new leaders and a great refresher for those of us experienced enough to require an occasional reminder about our real mission. It is my hope that *The Leader's Charter* provides you with refreshed context for your role and an additional tool to help you in the development of leaders around you.

The Leader's Charter

> *Your primary role as a leader is to <u>create an environment</u> that facilitates high individual and team performance against company and industry standards, supports innovation in processes, programs and approaches, encourages collaboration where necessary for objective achievement and promotes the development of your associates in roles that leverage their talents and interests and that challenge them to new and greater accomplishments.*

With apologies for the run-on sentence, I believe that *The Charter* captures the essence of the leader's reason for existence. It is an effective reminder of where your focus and energy should be placed and how you should gauge your progress and ultimately, your success. This is bedrock for your professional reason-for-being, and should define your high level goals and objectives as well as serve as a constant reminder of how you should be investing your time. Of course, *The Charter* is only as effective as you are committed to living up to its noble and achievement oriented philosophy.

Use The Leader's Charter to Ensure Focus on the Right Priorities

As you may already sense, the pace and demands of the work environment can be all consuming. It is possible to show up early, work late and never focus on the challenges inherent in *The Charter* as you pursue the transactional demands that bombard you on a daily basis. I have watched many an intelligent person fall victim to the tyranny of the urgent unimportant and completely lose sight of their core responsibility as a leader. In one case, a CEO confided to me his frustration over the apparent inability of an otherwise capable sales manager to do a better job developing his team and improving performance. I suggested to the CEO that he spend time observing how this manager spent his days interacting with and supporting his team. The CEO was amazed at how the transactional nature of the sales manager's approach precluded spending time on either the people-development component of his job or anything more strategic than the next deal. When the CEO asked the sales manager how he found time to focus on developing his team and driving performance improvements, his answer highlighted the core problem. "I don't. I help my team land deals and make numbers. It's what I like to do, and I am sure that you and the board want the numbers. I leave the other stuff to you and to marketing." The sales manager's honest answer spoke volumes. It clearly showed that he misunderstood his primary job as a leader and that he had no context for the responsibilities inherent in *The Charter*. In your own career as a leader, you will fight the tyranny of the urgent unimportant everyday. Use *The Leader's Charter* to establish and anchor your priorities!

Creating the Effective Environment—Some Practical Ideas to Help You On Your Journey

As a leader, you have a remarkable opportunity to create the team and environment that you believe are optimal for the current and expected challenges. Creating the effective environment is the artistic part of leadership and like great works of art, it resists replication by simple "how to" or step-by-step descriptions. It is as unlikely that Mozart could have guided people to replicate his genius through *A Guidebook to Becoming a Musical Prodigy,* any more than Churchill could have offered up, *The Handbook to Leading a Country During Near-Brushes With the End of Civilization.* Fortunately for you, your task is not quite as complex as the challenges that Mozart or Churchill might have faced, and there are some common-sense suggestions and approaches to help you create an effective work environment.

What defines the right environment varies by time and circumstances

During the course of a career you will likely deal with the challenges of growth and the challenge to grow. Both are very different with their own unique sets of problems and opportunities. The type of team, the talent mix, the tone and sense of urgency and the operating characteristics that work in one setting will likely not work in the other. As we highlighted in Chapter 4, it is critical that your efforts are grounded in a solid understanding of your organization's market situation, strategies and objectives. The outward facing view establishes the mission and then you build your team and environment to execute the mission in front of you. Of course, markets move quickly, competitors come and go and disruptive events and forces can dictate changes to a firm's game plan overnight. You need to stay grounded in what is happening externally to ensure that your own mission, team and approach are appropriate for the circumstances. An organization with a robust strategy and market monitoring process makes this task easier for the firm's line management. Lacking a robust market monitoring process, your best bet is to actively engage members of external facing teams to develop an understanding of what is going on in the marketplace. Casual conversations with sales or marketing reps or more formal invites for these individuals to update your team can ensure that you stay current with the market situation and can balance that against the team, approaches and environment that you are developing and leading.

Your style determines the characteristics of the environment

As we have talked about throughout the book, you have a powerful affect on the people around you through your words and actions. As a leader, everything that you do is magnified by peoples' observation and interpretations of what you are doing and saying, and you must leverage this power to define the characteristics of your team's working environment. Chapter 6 emphasized the importance of establishing and strengthening your credibility to gain the much-needed support of your team and other stakeholders across the organization. Without this personal credibility and believability, people may work for you to hold a job, but they will not work with you in creating a great team and driving great results. Seek every opportunity to strengthen your personal credibility through your approach, your honesty, your positive ethics and your respect for each and every member of your team. Remember, people want to be led by individuals that they believe in and that they trust. The working environment around a leader that has a high degree of credibility is much different than that of someone who lacks this important attribute. Your credibility is your currency as a leader.

Every team needs a goal!

Your ability to articulate and reinforce a vision and mission for the team and department (in line with the organization's vision and mission) will provide context for the work of your team and for the work environment at a point in time. Clear context is critical to the creation of an effective working environment. It is human nature to seek purpose in our activities, and when we internalize the purpose and believe that our own efforts can contribute to an overarching reason-for-being, we tend to provide the best that we have. Absence of a purpose creates apathy, reinforces the status quo and instills a sense of pointlessness that causes us to wander and get-by with as little effort as possible. It amazes me how many top executives don't get this and either provide vague visions of where the firm is going or instead focus on numbers as a reason for being.

In the absence of a clear organization vision, you must provide context for your team as part of your environment formation. Lacking appropriate guidance from your manager, set context for your team by establishing and working towards meaningful objectives to improve efficiency, reduce costs, and better serve internal or external customers or to confound competitors. Anything that serves to create a "reason for being" for your team and contributes to the improvement and ultimate success of your firm is appropriate when you lack guidance from on high.

In circumstances where the group needs a jolt, creating a crisis can be a powerful short-term motivator. Often, you do not have to look far to identify a crisis. A competitor's recent product announcement, a new market entrant or potential governmental regulation all can serve as legitimate catalysts to a crisis that will provide people context for their efforts. Remember, vision provides context and people and teams require context to perform at a high level.

Your commitment to paying attention to your team strengthens the work environment

The power of paying attention is remarkable. Chapter 8 will build on this theme in more detail, but suffice it to say that your associates want you to know what and how they are doing with their current challenges. They want your buy-in on their priority lists and they want to share their victories and seek your counsel on their challenges. Your willingness to pay attention is the ultimate sign of respect, and the notion that "you care" will contribute positively to building a dynamic and results-oriented work environment. Alternatively, if the tyranny of the urgent-unimportant takes hold of your agenda and keeps you from engaging with your associates in a quality manner, you are sabotaging your own efforts in creating an effective work environment.

Use your response to adversity as a means to strengthen the work environment

How you handle adversity, respond to alternative viewpoints and react to failures or setbacks has a powerful impact on the work environment. A leader that executes associates (in public or private) for failure, breeds all sorts of dysfunction, including fear, aversion to risk-taking and poor communications processes. Alternatively, a leader that leverages mistakes or failure as learning opportunities contributes to a culture of innovation, appropriate risk-taking and open communications. The leader that is self-confident enough to showcase their own failures as learning lessons for all makes significant contributions to their credibility account and reinforces the positive work environment that they are creating.

How you deal with poor performers is an important determinant of the effective environment

As a leader you will be faced with teams and individuals that struggle to learn from their mistakes and perhaps even repeat them. A positive response to people and teams failing in pursuit of innovation or audacious goals is very different from the managerial response you will need to take with poor performers. Your ability to identify when to eliminate chronic poor performers is equally important to your credibility and to your positive work environment creation. Support a poor performer too long and you weaken your credibility and others' interest in overachieving. Eliminate a poor performer with due process, fairness and everyone's best interests at heart and you again contribute to your credibility account. Adversity provides a golden opportunity for you to build credibility and strengthen the work environment. Leverage it aggressively.

Time is a powerful ally and enemy in the environment—use it carefully

Your understanding and judicious use of the clock and calendar in pursuit of building a great team and creating an effective work environment is important to your success. First, be aware that your direct manager likely has some perspective on the time frame for you to achieve the desired results. This position has a time to results quotient, and even if unstated, you cannot forget that you are on the clock. Wait too long to take action or drive results and your manager will lose confidence in your ability to lead. Move too fast and you risk creating excessive disruption and inviting a whole host of new problems. The process of gaining insight for your priorities and specifically for your manager's expectations for your results (including time frame) was covered in detail in Chapter 4. This understanding determines the pace of your activities and the rate with which you are driving changes in people, processes, programs and structure. Make certain to understand your own time quotient as you go about building your team and creating the effective working environment.

Time sets context for your team more powerfully than almost any other variable. A crisis demands rapid response and can drive people to operate at a high level of performance for a short period of time. You can leverage or manufacture a crisis and galvanize a group to produce for some amount of time. Alternatively, a perpetual state of crisis can exhaust individuals and groups and actually reduce performance.

Your role as a leader is to ensure that your team understands what part of the game clock they are using at any point in time. The two-minute drill in football is very different from the management of the clock early in the first or second quarter. A constant two-minute drill is not sustainable, but variations in the pace and urgency, including occasional pushes to cover a lot of ground in a hurry is appropriate. Your thoughtful use of time can set the rhythm for your team.

Leverage your natural business cycle to manage the energy level of your team

Many businesses run in a cycle that includes budgeting/planning, market events (trade show season), new product launches, tax season, holiday season and end of month/quarter/year pushes to name just a few. You can leverage that cycle in your planning and expectation setting, including getting new products to market, launching new advertising campaigns etc. to galvanize performance. In between the peaks of activity, there are opportunities to let down just a bit, refresh on goals, focus on professional development and engage in lessons-learned discussions. Your ability to recognize your cycle and manage the pace is an important part of creating your work environment. Understanding that life cannot be a perpetual crisis shows your maturity as a leader and ensures that your team gains the opportunity to both charge towards great accomplishments and recharge for the next set of challenges.

Operational accountability is a powerful contributor to building an effective working environment

The capstone of this book will focus on creating an operationally excellent team. Without the right working environment, you have little chance of achieving this lofty goal, but it works in the opposite direction as well. Operating processes that are meaningful and timely contribute to creating a culture of accountability, and accountability is an important part of an effective environment.

As team leader, you are responsible for establishing the reporting/ reviewing/updating mechanisms, and these settings provide an opportunity to build or destroy credibility. An effective leader will ensure that the sessions are timely and meaningful. If the updates are group settings, good meeting management practices must prevail. A regular agenda, a clear understanding of meeting rules and a clear leader must be visible. The sessions should be conducted on a regular schedule and expectations for participation well communicated and understood. Over time, these sessions can be powerful informal motivators, as the public nature of the event(s) drives people to hit targets and live up to commitments versus being visible as missing targets. The effective leader will pay attention to the sessions and ensure that they are managed for productive output and also identify when changes to format or time frame are needed. Additionally, the effective manager will delegate elements of these sessions to team members to lead, providing opportunities for visibility and responsibility development.

Additional suggestions for ensuring that operating processes contribute to effective environment development include:

- Don't overwhelm individuals or the groups with reporting and meeting requirements, or the team will begin to report and meet but not work or achieve.
- Solicit input on how to improve and make the events or reports more meaningful.
- Thrift out the unnecessary events and reports. If you or others don't benefit then cut out the activity.
- Make certain that the focus does not become insular. Ensure that the activities/reports and agendas are based on corporate objectives and market-facing issues. Invite market-facing associates to update the group on a regular basis.
- People will invariably have schedule conflicts. If you have one or two "must attend unless you are dead or close to it" meetings, make certain that this is well understood.
- As highlighted above, get others to contribute to the sessions and begin shaping the agenda. The development of "don't want to miss" meetings is an order of magnitude better than "don't miss or else" meetings.
- Never give short shrift to a performance review. Schedule them, conduct them professionally like you care (because you do!) and realize how important they are to the people you are reviewing.

It's Nice To Be Nice, But Not Essential

Treating people with respect is never optional, but being nice is not essential to creating the effective work environment. Recently, I observed a new CEO of a global firm chastise his staff for their apparent discomfort in discussing tough issues. In private, he described the culture as "collegial," but expressed frustration to the effect that this friendly environment kept people from focusing on the real problems that the firm faced.

In history and business there are many examples of great leaders where the word "nice" would be the last word associated with that person. General Patton, Coach Vince Lombardi or former GE CEO Jack Welch are all often highlighted as examples of extraordinary leaders who led teams to remarkable accomplishments. While widely respected, it is likely that few would describe them as nice.

Nice is not a requirement for success as a leader, nor is it a requirement to build an effective environment. Honesty, clarity of vision, fairness and respect are essential. While some company cultures are friendlier than others, you have to develop your own style as a leader and adapt it to the conditions and team that you are leading at the time. While nice is not a requirement for effective leadership, neither is an approach that is patently not nice. A good rule of thumb is to engage your associates as you prefer to be engaged, remembering that treating people with respect is never an option; it is an absolute.

How to Tell When You Are Making Progress
Creating the Effective Environment

The best way to gauge your progress for creating an effective work environment is to observe the actions and behaviors of your team. While words can mislead, actions never lie.

You know that your hard work to create an effective work environment is on track when you can recognize some or all of *The Seven Indicators.*

The Seven Indicators of the Effective Work Environment

1. Individuals and the group display a great deal of pride, collaboration and cooperation to meet and exceed objectives.

2. Failure to meet or exceed objectives is met with healthy frustration that quickly gets channeled into "lessons-learned" and "what can we do better" discussions.

3. Regardless of individual roles, virtual teams spontaneously assemble to meet specific challenges and then dissolve once the challenges have been met.

4. The group becomes self-policing on quality, timeliness and standards of conduct.

5. Individuals and the group begin to challenge themselves to innovate and drive results beyond the standards set by management.

6. The group knows how to play and fight together without impacting their results for the mission at hand.

7. The output is truly innovative, effective and tied to achieving key corporate objectives.

If you can see some or all of *The Seven Indicators* at play with your team, you should be encouraged that you are on the right track. If not, take a long hard look at *The Leader's Charter* and the suggestions in this chapter, and redouble your efforts to support your team. This is not some management utopia—nice to dream about but impossible to achieve. This is about your ability as leader to commit to and focus on doing the things necessary for your team to learn, act, succeed and prosper. It is also about your success as a leader. The first step starts with your recognition that creating an effective work environment is your primary job.

Thoughts from Rich: Developing Your Own Style and Using Drama to Positive Effect

A very popular question in interviews is to ask the potential new boss to describe their leadership style. You can probably hear the boilerplate answers in your head. "I have a participative approach." "My door is always open." "I'm firm but fair." And in fairness to the leaders offering tired and worn-out answers to this important question, it can be difficult to describe your style. Most leaders do not think about their style, much less proactively develop one, but they should. The first step in developing your own style is to act like a leader. For some it comes naturally, but for most, it requires effort and practice.

Shakespeare wrote "All the world's a stage and all the men and women merely players. They have their exits and entrances, and one man in his time plays many parts..." Leaders in particular are always on stage, and the persona that they choose should be carefully tailored to the circumstances at the time and the message that they want to communicate to their team. And while you might rankle at the term, "act," I am by no means implying that you should attempt to deceive or be insincere. Rather, I am suggesting that the leader's approach to displaying emotion, to showing passion, fire, joy or frustration and dissatisfaction in the right way at the right time is a powerful tool in shaping behaviors and creating the effective work environment.

In times of crisis, a quiet confidence can calm the team and help them focus on problem solving. In times of success, the leader's display of genuine enthusiasm will communicate pride and happiness with the team. A leader's controlled display of dissatisfaction or annoyance can send a powerful message to the team, affecting behavior in the short and long term. If you think about an actor's ability to make their audience believe, you have the same goal as a leader. If you are upset about something it's ok to show it. If you are really pleased about the quality of a deliverable, show your pleasure.

How do you balance the appropriate use of drama with being yourself? There is no magic answer here. You can still be effective if your style is quiet and laid back, especially if you learn how to apply a bit of fire and brimstone at the appropriate time. Just the knowledge that you can transform from mild mannered leader to a passionate and outspoken zealot for truth, justice and getting things done the right way, will have a positive impact on your work environment and your team's effectiveness. In addition, you will be more successful in attracting desirable candidates to your team if prospects perceive some degree of verve in your style as a leader.

Early in my career I worked with a department head that had a reputation as a tyrant. If something in his area didn't get done on time, or there were quality or financial implications he would go off on the offending party. These outbursts were predictable–they didn't just happen. They included behaviors we would generally put into the category of tirade in the worst-case or perhaps highly animated in the best case. The object of his emotion was usually the benefactor of plenty of close attention for a short period of time following the episode. Once he understood that the problem was completely cleaned up, and it was clear to him that a lesson was learned such that the offending incident was not unlikely to be repeated, he would back off. Outside of these infrequent episodes he was an extremely affable, even gregarious person.

To be fair, he was also the first to acknowledge achievements when they occurred. He had a big smile, which he used to its full, infectious effect, and a manner of expressing his pleasure over positive outcomes that could only be perceived as warm, genuine appreciation. This behavior from him was revered as much as the alternative was feared.

The seemingly bi-polar nature of his behavior seemed odd to me – I didn't understand at the time why he was prone to these tirades when he largely behaved in such a normal way. His business results were phenomenal, but it seemed like he was incapable of managing his emotions. I learned later on that his use of emotion was a part of his leadership style and a component of the work environment that he sought to create and the behaviors that he wanted to shape. This was my first experience with somebody who took the stage to great effect, but not my last. In the years since it has been the rare exception to work with a leader who is great at what he or she does and who also doesn't have some ham in them.

The case is strong for brushing up on your dramatic persona, but before you take the stage for your next performance, remember that there are some definite pitfalls to avoid.

- *Like eating too much dessert, drama can quickly lost its appeal. Don't overdo it.*

- *Using highly demonstrative behavior with the wrong audience can backfire on you. Some individuals are so sensitive that overt displays of emotion may be perceived as intimidating to the point you squelch desirable behavior.*

- *You need to be sincere. Unless you are a skilled Hollywood actor or actress, your team will seize upon any insincerity as an opportunity to debit your credibility bank account.*

As with all of the skills presented in this book, practice makes perfect. You will find an opportunity or situation ripe for a little bit of drama almost every working day, so remember to put your skills to the test. Good luck, and break a leg!

-Rich

Epilogue

This chapter highlighted the importance of creating an effective working environment to your success as a leader. While the concept is intuitive, it is not necessarily front-of-mind as you fight day-to-day battles, nor is it easy to do. Many otherwise competent individuals derail on the leadership track because they do not internalize their responsibility to create the effective working environment, nor do they realize the power that they have to affect this environment.

The tyranny of the urgent unimportant can easily overwhelm anyone's agenda, and it takes discipline and insight to stay focused on your core responsibilities. *The Leader's Charter* provides a strong reminder of where your focus and energy should be applied, and what your primary responsibilities to your associates are at all times. An effective working environment has its roots in your personal and professional credibility as a leader as well as in your conduct and the articulation and reinforcement of your vision. The operating mechanisms for reporting and updating can be powerful tools in creating a culture of accountability. Your assurance that all activities are focused on building customer and market value further strengthens your environment by providing context for the activities of your associates. Time is a powerful tool that can be leveraged or abused and should be carefully managed to provide opportunities to both charge the hill and recharge the batteries.

Your success as a leader depends upon your ability to gain the trust and commitment of a group of people who are naturally wary to bestow their trust and commitment to people undeserving. Your credibility is core to building trust and your focus on creating an environment where people are treated fairly and with respect, encouraged to take risks and learn from mistakes and where professional and personal development are encouraged, will combine to produce an environment of innovation and achievement.

PRACTICAL LESSONS IN LEADERSHIP

Discussion Questions-Mark's Mess Gets Messier

- *Where should Mark start to try and sort his mess out?*
- *What action plan would you suggest for Mark to carry him through the next 60 days?*
- *How should he deal with his "hands off" boss?*

For ideas on how the authors view the situation at Apex and the issues outlined above, visit the Leadership Resource Center at www.management-innovations. com, and click on Practical Lessons-Discussion Questions.

PREFACE TO CHAPTER 8

SAM'S SURPRISE

Sam Jackson was glad that 360's were completed. This was the first year that Apex had used this technique for reviewing the performance of all leaders, and it had been nerve-wracking for some, but not for Sam. He prided himself on giving his people plenty of room to operate and in general, he stayed out of their business. More than a few people had indicated that they appreciated this about him.

He also understood why Victoria Pyott, the company's CEO had initiated this program. Apex wasn't going to reinvigorate itself unless the leadership team led the charge. Frankly, Sam thought that this new review program might just weed out a few of the leaders that weren't as committed as they should be.

The envelope marked "confidential" contained the feedback for Sam, and after grabbing a fresh cup of coffee he sat down and prepared to see what the team had to say about him. Truthfully, he felt there were at least a few points that he could learn from. He knew that his "If I'm successful, you're successful, so stay out of my way and handle things," philosophy worked, but after all, everyone could improve.

Sam took the first sip from his fresh cup of coffee and tore into the envelope. By the time he reached for the cup again, the coffee had grown cold.

"Too distant to be of much help," read one of the reviews. "Doesn't understand the challenges that we have in front of us," and "Gives us plenty of room, but always seems too busy to be bothered by departmental business," read another. "Don't know what he wants from us or what our direction for the future should be," "Wish Sam would offer more than cheerleading," and "I don't think he has any idea about the strengths, weaknesses or aspirations of his teammates," indicated the last review.

After the comments, he reviewed the scores and the news was the same. Low marks for overall leadership strength, coaching and directing. And perhaps the most disturbing of all, the morale ranking for his team averaged a 2 out of 5, with 5 being the best. Sam was shocked.

CHAPTER 8
THE POWER OF PAYING ATTENTION
TO YOUR PEOPLE

I once inherited a team previously managed by a person that fit the "too busy" profile that we outlined in Chapter 6. This manager reportedly filled her days with conference calls and meetings, but somehow never seemed to have time to meet with her team members about their ideas, concerns or to provide counsel on their professional development. A number of her former staffers indicated that is seemed like she was afraid of those types of discussions, and as such, she avoided them as much as possible. Paying attention was not a part of this manager's style.

As I assumed responsibility for this team, I sensed that many of the individuals were frustrated with the prior manager's style. There seemed to be an attention deficit that needed repairing, but I did not fully realize how bad the situation was until I began talking with everyone. Immediately following my promotion, I took my own advice and kicked into gear with the start-up suggestions outlined in Chapter 5. I set up team sessions to introduce myself and to get people talking about themselves and their projects. I committed to a series of one-hour sessions over the next few weeks with each of the team members and I communicated the agenda in advance, outlining the questions that I would be asking and highlighting my need to hear the unadulterated version of what we needed to do to improve the team and hit our targets. I then proceeded to follow through on my commitment to meet with everyone, and the feedback staggered me!

I've never experienced anything in my career quite like the reaction that I received during that initial round of discussions. It was as if my gesture of investing time to personally meet with and listen to people was some rare gift that I was providing. People actually cried, most sent me long thank you notes or e-mails and I was truly humbled to think that a bit of my time was worth so much to anyone, much less important enough to merit an outpouring of emotion. I learned a lot through that experience. I learned that I had some remarkably talented people who had gone unchallenged and underdeveloped for several years. I was reminded of the human need to be treated with respect, and that my time and attention was the highest order of respect that I could pay a person. Ultimately, we led a sweeping reorganization focused on a major new strategy initiative, and many of these individuals found themselves with fresh challenges and a new lease on their career. Together, we generated record results two years in a row under some remarkably challenging circumstances.

Why Paying Attention is Essential

It is hard to write this chapter and not think that I am telling you that breathing is essential to effective leadership, not to mention survival. Having come this far in the book and having suffered through my opening anecdote in this chapter, you will have to trust that the leaders that are truly good at paying attention to their people are far outnumbered by various derivatives of the "too busy" manager. Consider the impact on your credibility, your environment and ultimately your team's results if you adopt the too-busy approach. If you're too busy to pay attention, bad things happen. For example:

- You frustrate your associates who are working hard to meet their objectives and may require your input or at times a decision that will allow them to solve a critical problem.

- You disrespect your associates as professionals by indirectly communicating that their needs/perspectives are secondary to your priorities. This reduces your credibility and ultimately your effectiveness.

- You lose touch with the dynamics of your environment.

- You miss chances to identify individual or team development needs/opportunities
- You shoot down any element of loyalty that your people might have felt towards you.
- You create an air of malaise with your team. If you don't care, why should they?
- You fail to recognize a basic human need for visibility and as a result demoralize those that seek your understanding and acknowledgement.
- You do a disservice to your firm and ultimately to your own career.

Alternatively, if you do a good job paying attention to your people, good things happen. Just a few of these include:

- People see that you care...about their work and their challenges and this "caring" creates a sense of importance, urgency and pride. You build credibility and loyalty by caring.
- You show respect to people as professionals and human beings, and respect is a powerful motivator.
- You develop and maintain a keen understanding of what is going on in your work environment and what part of your program is working or not working.
- You identify opportunities for team and individual development, ultimately reinforcing that you care about people as professionals. Your commitment to strengthening people's skill sets and providing growth opportunities positively affects credibility, loyalty and ultimately performance.
- You strengthen your environment by infusing accountability into the equation. People understand that they will be updating you and the group on activities and that alone can drive increased aggressiveness in pursuit of objectives. This energy is infectious.
- You meet the basic need that many have for visibility, further strengthening your credibility.
- You create more effective communications processes and ideally a comfort in talking about and resolving tough topics. These improved communication processes are critical to realizing effective problem-solving as well as catalyzing a culture of innovation.
- You are doing your job!

Hopefully by now, you get the point. Building a great team requires care and feeding from the leader, and providing your time (in the right manner) is the most powerful tool at your disposal. The "too-busy" bosses of the world don't comprehend the negative impact that their approach has on the organization and their direct associates. Now, you do, and you can leverage this knowledge to distance yourself from chronic under-performing leaders as you develop your team and grow your career.

What Do We Mean By "Paying Attention?"

Simple question but not such a simple answer. You could easily misinterpret my imploring you to pay attention as the need to maintain a constant open door and a willingness to drop everything and listen to anything an associate had to say at any point in time. In fact, nothing could be further from the truth. As you gain experience leading and managing teams, you will find that some people are remarkably adept at wasting their own and everyone else's time with their issues or opinions. If you let them, these individuals will suck every available second from you, distracting you from focusing on the real issues and challenges of the day. Recall that in Chapter 4 we highlighted a number of potential pitfalls and obstacles that you will encounter in dealing with people, including:

- Everyone has an agenda
- Their personal problems can become your management challenges
- You will spend too much time with the wrong people

These are real issues for you as a leader and you will need to develop effective early warning and filtering systems to ensure that your agenda is not dominated by these time-killers. One solution is to take a proactive approach to paying attention, by creating forums and communications opportunities to engage people and solicit their insights and updates. As referenced constantly throughout this book, your creation of the forums for feedback, insight, input, brainstorming and problem solving are essential to your success as a leader

Building an Effective Personal Communications Program:

The development and publication of your personal communications program is an important part of building an effective communications culture with your team. As a new leader, you need to understand what's going on in the minds of your team members, and they certainly want to know what's going on in yours. A change in leadership is generally associated with a heightened state of concern as people wonder what this change will mean for their role and even their continued employment. And while you as the new leader will absolutely be evaluating the talent on your team, the faster you establish and communicate your start-up agenda and turn the focus of the team to the right business priorities, the faster you will begin generating the results that your company is expecting from you.

An effective personal communication program incorporates all of the following key ingredients:

1. One-on-One introductions
2. Active and visible reinforcement
3. Consistency and accountability
4. Informal opportunities

One-on-One Introductions

In Chapter 5, we discussed a number of kick-off meetings that are important when you step into a new role. For this section, we will focus on the personal communications component at start-up, and then incorporate some group activities as we move into creating regular contact meetings where business priorities and results are visible to all.

At start-up of a new leadership role, it is essential to touch everyone as quickly as possible. Assuming the size of the team allows for reasonable one-on-one communications, it is important to let everyone know that you will be talking with them personally during the upcoming few weeks. I have done this with teams from four to seventy, and although the larger the team, the more the strain on your schedule, there is nothing more important than leveraging this unique point in time to gain insights and to begin establishing your leadership credibility.

You should communicate your agenda in advance, and then be relentless about scheduling and keeping the appointments. Your advance notice of the agenda topics and your follow-through in conducting the discussions will create a positive energy throughout your entire team. In my own experience, I have found that the simpler the agenda for this first contact meeting the better, so I use the following *Kick-off Questions:*

1. What's working?
2. What's not working?
3. How should we improve?
4. What do you want/expect from me?
5. What do you want to do in this organization?

These conversation starters help break the ice with your associates and place the focus on topics that are important to them, including their ideas, their careers and what they want from you as a leader. When conducting the discussions, remember the 2:1 ratio (two ears, one mouth, use them in proportion)! These sessions are for listening and observing more than talking. You will have ample opportunity to be heard in the future.

Active and visible reinforcement

Your commitment to meeting or talking with your associates is important, but your willingness to truly listen and understand the issues, as well as identify opportunities for follow-up establishes your approach to leadership. Whether you are conducting start-up conversations or general operations discussions, you should seek opportunities to commit to follow-up with your associates and then live up to that commitment. Nothing shows that you care more than conscientious and timely follow-up. Alternatively, nothing shows that you don't care more than blowing off commitments to follow-up, or worse yet, never being willing to even consider following-up. One of my "favorite" managers had a habit of responding to issues by stating, "that is truly important and we should deal with it at the right time." It was never the right time and his people knew it.

Regular contact through operations reviews and team updates

Whether you are assuming responsibility for a new team or reinvigorating your communications program with your current team, your commitment to timely and regular group and individual contact is essential to building a culture of accountability and reinforcing your commitment to paying attention. Two forums that are essential to running your business or team and that ensure that everyone is on the same page with priorities and goals include the *Quarterly Operations Review* and the *Monthly Team Update*.

The *Quarterly Operations Review* should include your direct reports and focus on a detailed review of progress against objectives as well as planning for the upcoming quarter. This is a "must attend" meeting, and your communication that an absence requires prior approval, a written note from their mother and a walk across hot coals, is important to letting everyone understand that you are serious. Key suggested agenda topics for this meeting include:

Quarterly Operations Review Agenda

- Progress against objectives and actions to ensure successful completion
- Operating metrics review and analysis discussion
- Changes in environment/market/industry/company that affect strategy
- New/additional objectives identification, prioritization and ownership
- Talent/staff development needs/issues

As the leader, you need to ensure that the agenda is developed and distributed ahead of time, that your team leaders are providing relevant updates, and that the meeting is managed to ensure agenda completion, with minimal wandering around the proverbial forest. Always identify a note-taker and timekeeper, and make certain to shift those roles from session to session. One additional suggestion to add variety to the agenda and to provide a learning opportunity for everyone is to assign an advance reading on a relevant leadership or industry topic and facilitate a discussion with the entire group. However, beware the tendency to jam too much into the agenda. The focus that you place on the key issues and your commitment to a regular meeting schedule reinforces your focus on the business and the people. You are paying attention.

The sixty minute *Monthly Team Update* is for everyone under your umbrella, and is an opportunity to update the team on progress against objectives, review highlights and challenges of the prior period, and importantly, plan for the upcoming period. I enjoyed watching one of my favorite sales managers use these monthly meetings to update the entire selling and supporting organization on prior month's results, communicate next month's targets and to provide previews of coming attractions. Also, the sales manager leveraged this forum to provide visibility on accomplishments, including wins, competitor drubbings and great individual and team heroics in support of customers. What a powerful way to reinforce your objectives, show your focus on the business and key issues and provide visibility to your high performers. One caveat. Many managers complain about the complexity of time zones and geography as barriers to this meeting. There are many inexpensive solutions for recording and broadcasting or making the meeting available for viewing on-demand, so time and distance should not pose a barrier to conducting and attending these important and powerful sessions.

The Power of Informal Communications

Informal communications opportunities are remarkably valuable in gaining insight into people and issues, and you should leverage this powerful tool as part of your overall communications program. In addition to setting and keeping a formal meeting schedule, I love to create "drive-by" opportunities to reach out and see how people are doing or ask them what's going on. My favorite approach was a "Friday phone-call" with individual members of one of my operations teams to rehash the week's achievements and talk about upcoming activities. These were casual, no stress calls and often included an inquiry about the upcoming weekend. We frequently discussed what we had learned this week and often brainstormed on a new project or program to help us achieve our objectives. These opportunities also provided the team members with a forum to offer suggestions or to bounce their ideas around. I knew that they had become institutionalized whenever schedules would force me to miss my Friday rounds and on Monday morning my e-mail inbox would include a few "Hey, where were you on Friday?" notes. Regardless of how, where or when, the important point is for you to create informal opportunities to interact with your associates. Managed properly, you can learn a lot through these drive-by interactions.

Establishing a regular communications protocol

Your team wants to understand how to communicate with you. You need to establish and publish a communications protocol, and then live up to it. If you voice an open-door policy, then your door better be open and you approachable more often than not. I prefer to establish semi-formal time slots for my key managers where we engage daily or several times per week and important but non-urgent issues are saved for these sessions. In the past I've talked with a sales manager every night before heading home and my sales engineering head every morning before things kicked into gear. I set up more frequent regular contact time for newer managers and less frequent but still formal time for my more experienced and independent team leaders.

Emergencies happen, and when one breaks out, your team needs to know how to cut through your calendar and gain your full attention. Ensure that you have established a clear 911 protocol, including a reasonable definition of what constitutes an emergency and what does not. When the alarm bell rings, you need to shift gears and engage immediately!

If you work in an e-mail culture, create a semi-regular communiqué outlining targets, prior period results, successes and new initiatives. Just make certain that when it lands in everyone's in-box, it has value, otherwise you risk diluting your communications effectiveness. In managing a sales team, I found value in leveraging this slightly more impersonal form of communications during the middle of the selling month and about two weeks following our team call. The e-mail provided me an opportunity to remind everyone of monthly targets, closing dates and other administrative issues, as well as to provide visibility in print to reps or teams that had landed a big deal or put out a major fire.

As you move beyond the start-up phase of a leadership role, remember to sanity check your communications approach with your managers and your associates. Are there too many meetings? Too few? Do the communiqués inform or are they ignored? What else do people want or need to hear? All of these are valid questions that you should ask your team as a means of improving your communications effectiveness, and to show that you are truly paying attention. You will be amazed at the great ideas and feedback that you get from your associates.

Are You Really Paying Attention?

Several years ago I had the good fortune to attend an Executive Development course at Northwestern's Kellogg Graduate School, entitled, *Reinventing Leadership: A Breakthrough Approach*. The course instructors, Pierre Casse and Paul Claudel who taught this course at Kellogg (in addition to serving other institutions) suggested that all people have a Project To Live (PTL) which consists of some deeply personal priorities, and that a person's PTL at a point in time would govern their approach to their lives and their work. With apologies to Pierre and Paul for gross oversimplification, a person's PTL changes over the course of a lifetime, usually dictated by a life stage or by significant events. As a young professional, your priorities might include career growth, money, travel and diversity of assignments, and as a mid-career professional, the list or priorities might read family, faith, security and stability. Pierre and Paul submit that to be an effective leader, you need to understand a person's PTL and to use this insight as a means of helping them develop or produce. Of course, the catch here is that it is quite awkward (as well as potentially illegal) to ask someone the probing questions needed to get a read on their PTL. The reality is that if you are doing what we are suggesting in this book: creating the environment, ensuring timely and proper communications, treating people with respect and living up to *The Leader's Charter* and visiting informally, you have the opportunity to learn a lot about a person without asking awkward or potentially litigious questions. If you are an astute listener, you will begin to understand what individuals view as important and how they set their priorities. A career oriented person will communicate in many ways their desire to grow, to be challenged and to advance, while a person more concerned about quality time with family will shy away from discretionary travel and extraordinary assignments that will soak up time off. The moral to this story is that people are much more than what you see in the office, and your ability to look for and attempt to understand their priorities or PTL will aid you in helping them be successful.

Epilogue

The anecdote at the beginning of the chapter is going to help me tie things off here at the end. Never in my career have I received a more powerful message than during that few weeks when I followed the plan and talked with and listened to some very frustrated but remarkably talented people. At times it was easy for me to think that I was doing something akin to setting people free from some form of tyranny, but then my common-sense would knock my ego over the head and remind me that anyone in my position that chooses to listen would have had the same effect. Ultimately, we made many changes in the team—some were promoted and some were fired, and the remaining, re-energized group knocked down more obstacles than any team deserved to face in an eighteen-month period. I was fortunate to support them, and all I had to do to set things in motion was pay attention.

As you grow your career and take on the responsibility of creating an effective leadership development culture for managers reporting to you, remember to pay the lessons of this chapter forward. Make certain that your leaders understand the importance of paying attention, that they establish their own personal communications program, and that they are relentless in reinforcing effective communications practices through timely and consistent group and individual forums. As I said earlier in the book, the role of a leader would be easy if it were not for the people. Fortunately, people are what we have. Listen to your people and learn. It's your job.

Discussion Questions-Sam's Surprise

- *How could Sam be so out of touch with how people viewed his leadership effectiveness?*
- *Why might Sam's people have been uncomfortable addressing this with him personally prior to the new 360-degree review process?*
- *How should Sam respond to his team members?*
- *Describe the program that you would suggest for Sam to rehabilitate his leadership style.*
- *Can Sam be saved?*

For ideas on how the authors view the situation at Apex and the issues outlined above, visit the Leadership Resource Center at www.management-innovations. com, and click on Practical Lessons-Discussion Questions.

PREFACE TO CHAPTER 9

JULIE'S TEAM COULD DO NO WRONG

Pat Paulsen, Customer Support Director at Apex, turned her attention to the stack of performance reviews prepared by Julie Trip, the Technical Support Team Leader. Pat enjoyed having Julie on her team. She was good at her job and her team members enjoyed working for her. Pat's only concern with Julie was her inability to provide constructive feedback to her team members. Last year's reviews from Julie were filled with great comments and the scores were out of the ballpark. The constructive issues that needed addressing were absent from the reviews, and Julie had confessed to Pat that she had a difficult time delivering constructive feedback. Pat hoped that the full day seminar on conducting effective performance reviews that Julie had attended would improve the quality of this year's reports.

As Pat closed the file folder containing Julie's reviews, she sighed. According to Julie, every member of her team had exceeded expectations in every aspect of their performance. The majority of the comments were incredibly positive, with a few weak attempts at some developmental comments sprinkled throughout the documents. "Julie must have slept through the training," thought Pat, wondering what she could do to help her get over her fear of giving feedback.

Alan Discovers Karma

Fred Bauer had just finished a tough discussion with Alan Michaels and he felt good. Fred knew that he had postponed this for too long, in part because he knew it would be contentious, and in part because Alan operated in a gray area, never overtly stepping over the line. However, the issue with Sharon was the last straw.

It had taken Fred a few years to see the pattern in Alan's approach. Whenever things were tough for Alan's team, Alan would carefully work in an issue about someone else or some other team, and Fred cringed when he realized that this technique had worked on him a few times. However, Alan's repeated shots at Sharon were too visible to ignore, and particularly because Sharon and Fred had long ago agreed on an action plan to help Sharon manage her issues and still keep the team cranking. Alan's lousy results and his not very nice technique of stabbing his peers in the back, while smiling, were no longer acceptable.

Alan's reaction to Fred's very clear and direct feedback was surprising. Instead of a fight, Alan had broken down. Alan acknowledged that his approach was wrong, and asked for a second chance.

CHAPTER 9
"NO ONE EVER TOLD ME THAT BEFORE."
LEVERAGING FEEDBACK AS A
POWERFUL LEADERSHIP TOOL

I am willing to bet Art's lunch money for the week that you have <u>not</u> been in a situation where your boss presented a nugget of feedback that caused you to offer that response. Unless you have been fortunate enough to have a great manager, or maybe you have participated in a 360-degree feedback exercise where peers and internal customers can share provocative comments under the veil of anonymity, you may have heard watered down items that were only remotely candid or useful. On one hand you may be thankful for the lack of candor, but in the end, coming up short on feedback – particularly corrective feedback - shortchanges everybody involved: you, your manager, your team members and the organization. In this chapter we will give you the insight needed to become comfortable and confident in having candid discussions with your associates.

While we have the wagering theme going, I am also willing to bet you that right after public speaking, giving feedback to another person – and in this context let's assume we are referring to corrective feedback – is the most dreaded task imaginable. Further, I'm also willing to bet that the reason this fear has perpetuated in human beings to this day is that our experience as receivers of feedback is largely made up of bad examples. Everything from clouding the true message with euphemistic language to pure avoidance has fanned the flames of fear around this topic. One last bet – it doesn't have to be this way, and you can turn this fear into a key strength.

A Brief Description of Feedback

Many of the terms we use in organizational life these days have inherent meaning that we assume are universally understood, but may not be. Feedback in this context includes all of the messages you deliver about how somebody is doing. As a percentage of your time, leaders will often deliver positive guidance and acknowledgment for results, but the more challenging – albeit less frequent - situations involve opportunities to provide course corrections. The settings run the gamut of "drive-bys" which are the brief conversations you deliver on an ad hoc basis when passing in the hall, meeting in the lunchroom, etc. to the evaluation you deliver in an annual performance review. The important point here is that leaders are constantly evaluating and playing back what they see and hear for the benefit of the individuals, the team and the organization. Just ask yourself this question: how will your people know how they are doing today if they don't hear it from you?

A Whole Chapter on Feedback?

As a new leader you may understand that providing feedback is an important part of your job, and it's important to do it well. But is it worth a dedicated chapter? Your authors certainly feel it is, and by the end of this chapter we believe you will agree with us. From our perspective, the two most powerful tools that leaders have to shape behavior of the people around them are setting expectations and providing feedback. All your energy, desire, and credibility will be useless if you can't convert those attributes into actions. Your feedback skill as a manager determines not only how effective you are at communicating your expectations but also how well you are able to guide behavior once those expectations are set.

Profound implications for the organization regarding the practice of feedback came to light during the research interviews we conducted for this book. After considering the results as a whole we saw a spider web of connections that feedback has with many facets of organizational life. Consider the following responses from our research interviews:

- A majority of managers reported they lacked confidence in their own ability to deliver corrective feedback effectively.

- Managers were reluctant to engage when a correction was needed, which underscored the biggest leadership mistake reported by our participants – acting too slowly on a performance problem. This reluctance to act is a reasonable outcome when leaders lack confidence in their skills.

- Leaders routinely wished their own managers were better with feedback. When we asked about the source of the most valuable feedback they have received, we heard that it came from peers, subordinates and personal development seminars as often as their manager.

- Interviewees told us there was little, if any, frank guidance provided to them as new managers, yet they universally believed the most powerful thing the organization can do to help first-time leaders to be effective is routine feedback and coaching.

These are not difficult clues to follow. They tell us that feedback is tied to many desirable outcomes for people and organizations, yet it is amazingly elusive in practice. The more we thought about it, it seemed that feedback behavior is analogous to a circle that encompasses and connects so many things that happen in an organization. Feedback shapes individual behavior, which in turn drives desired results. Feedback establishes objectives for personal development that creates highly knowledgeable individual contributors and skilled leaders that are necessary for the organization to evolve. Senior management relies on feedback from all levels to help the organization evolve its capabilities relative to its strategy plan. As new capabilities evolve, the circle completes itself and starts over with new or revised expectations at the individual level. You can visualize that in the absence of feedback, or when the skill level is generally deficient, you will have people in constant motion who look busy on the surface, but are not really headed in a common direction. If the direction is unclear, you don't have to waste any time assessing the quality of results!

The area of feedback is a fertile topic among training and development professionals, and has been the subject of numerous books. We'll provide a broad overview in this chapter to make sure you have a great foundation on which to build, but don't think your learning ends here. For those of you with the interest and commitment to earn your wings in *Feedback Mastery* check out the Seminars and Workshops area of our website at www.management-innovations.com.

A Message from Human Resources about Feedback

Before we get too deep into this subject, I have to include a brief commercial regarding the need for you to follow routines established by your human resources function regarding your recordkeeping for these conversations. They will no doubt have a protocol for if and when you document these conversations and how to do it, so if you are not already up to speed on those procedures see your manager or somebody in human resources for guidance. Don't expect that you will have to write up everything you say to each of your team members, but cases moving towards demoting or firing somebody will require thorough and proper documentation. The working and legal worlds today favor the prepared and documented manager – it is rarely as simple as who is right and wrong.

The First Step – Categorizing the Situation

The first thing you should do to manage a corrective feedback situation is determine the nature of the problem and pair that up with the approach that best suits that circumstance. The following model illustrates four distinct situational categories (combinations of willing and able represented by the axes) and the feedback approach (identified in the numbered boxes) that is best suited to each situation. As you probably realize, people and circumstances aren't so tidy or discreetly categorized, and the model represents this as a continuum for each axis. We will offer guidance for these broad categories, but realize your approach may require tweaking to best fit your needs at the time.

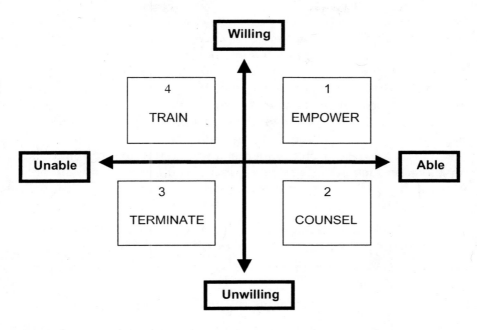

Box 1: Willing, Able

Life is good in this situation. Your focus here is to identify opportunities to reinforce current good behavior and provide coaching for developmental purposes. If you do notice behavior that needs to be corrected with somebody in this category it will only take a minute of your time. Literally. Make your point, describe the preferred behavior and move on with no deep philosophical discussion required. More importantly, find something challenging for this person to do and get out of the way!

- "Thanks for making sure that quote got in the mail before end of business yesterday. It was a late request so I know it required some extra effort." OR

- "Before you submit those benefits reports you should take an extra minute to double check your numbers since the impact of a mistake like yesterday's can be significant."

Box 2: Unwilling, Able

Your intervention skills will be tested in this case, where you goal is to positively influence somebody who has the ability, but seems to be choosing not to meet your expectations. Do you have the skill to positively influence somebody who willingly chooses to go the other direction? What latitude do you have to act? We will walk you through an approach for managing this situation, but please remember that each case will be different and that you will only get better at this with practice and experience.

Your first objective is to describe the behavior you feel depicts the unwillingness and contrast it with your standing expectations and perhaps the person's prior conduct. The important term here is behavior – you must make your observation in a way that it doesn't sound like an attack on the person. Further, because willingness is not tangible you will have to rely on your own good judgment to make this call. For example:

- "I noticed you have not been asking questions in the morning production meetings for the past week or so." OR
- "The weekly sales analysis is taking longer and longer to complete." NOT
- "I don't think you care about the production meetings anymore."

Whatever the aberration is you have to be able to describe it as succinctly as possible. If this is a situation that doesn't require a written correction, you may still find that writing down your observation beforehand makes it easier to be clear and to the point.

Your next step is to find out why the person is unwilling, and we often describe this approach as counseling. Counseling is typified by a robust dialog – very much a two-way street - in order to understand and assess the likely source of the unwillingness. Again, if this person otherwise has the ability, it is worth some investment to assess and fix the unwillingness. This is going to be as straight-forward as you are probably imagining right now…you have to ask the "why" question and do it with some degree of finesse so it doesn't sound like a personal attack. If you're too heavy-handed you will slam the door on potential dialog and then have no data to work with beyond your observation.

- "Is there a reason you have not been as involved in the meetings as you have in the past?" OR
- "Why has it been taking longer to complete the sales analysis?"

Be prepared that the source of the unwillingness may not be work related, such as a lack of motivation at the present time due to marital difficulties, stress from the burden of medical care for a sick family member, or maybe the person is contemplating a career change. If the origin is work related, such as a problem with another associate, you can address that problem directly. If the source is a personal, non work-related issue like one of the examples above, it may require some creative problem solving on your part. You should break the meeting and agree to continue the dialog once you have had a chance to confer with your manager and perhaps human resources to kick around ideas, understand what additional resources may be available and confirm what latitude you have to act. Can you adjust work schedules or authorize some paid time off? Do you have an Employee Assistance Plan or something similar that provides support for employees with personal issues? The underlying principle at this stage is that you show empathy for the personal issue, offer to help if that is appropriate, but make it clear that the behavior must change regardless of how the personal problem works out.

- "You will make an appointment with the academic counselor at Community Tech to learn about admission requirements for the Network Program, and if it requires time off during the day we will make an effort to adjust your schedule so you don't have to miss work. Starting tomorrow I will count on you to be engaged in the production meeting like the rest of the team." OR

- "Your plan is to call your pastor for a referral to a marriage counselor in an attempt to see if you can preserve your marriage and to help you deal with the feelings you are having as a result. In the meantime you will make an effort to participate in the morning meeting like the rest of the team." OR

- "I can appreciate that you don't like working with Jake, but the report still needs to be completed accurately and on time. I will work with Jake to make sure you have the sales data by end of business Thursday so you can have the analysis reports completed and distributed by Monday at noon."

A final principle to remember here is that you cannot make resolution of a personal problem a condition of employment or a reason to formally correct an associate, but the <u>performance issue</u> that seems to result from the personal problem is definitely your call. With guidance from your manager and experience in dealing with these situations, you will develop a sense of judgment regarding how much accommodation is appropriate and how much to press on the behavior change.

These cases are worthy of some investment on the organization's behalf, assuming the ability is there. Tenure and past performance history should be factors in your decision about how much time, energy and expense to invest. You have influence but very little control over the outcome here – at least in terms of positively resolving the unwillingness. In the end you may be able to cajole the individual over to the willing side of the box, but if not, the subject is a candidate for termination.

Box 3: Unwilling, Unable

How did you end up with somebody in this category? As interesting as that question may be, the issue of the day is to resolve the problem. As with Box 2, you should start with understanding the unwillingness issue before spending too much energy on assessing ability. There may be some performance history that is documented, and if it is not positive you should spend very little of your valuable time on the unwillingness issue for obvious reasons. You also need to be sensitive to the fact that an ability issue may masquerade as a willingness issue if the associate doesn't have confidence in their skills. This can be difficult to determine, and you will likely have to rely on their peers for input here unless you have first hand exposure to their work on a daily basis. Refer to the verbiage for Box 2 as the first step in dealing with these cases until or unless you confirm the person is also unable.

As we have mentioned in earlier chapters, do not get sucked in to investing any more time than absolutely necessary in what may be your weakest resources. If you have an individual that you believe is both unwilling and unable, this is probably a candidate for termination. In rare cases somebody that has been misplaced (i.e. hired or promoted into a position for which they are not suited) may also look like an unwilling and unable case but be very careful here. You want to make sure the organization doesn't play checkers with what may be a questionable resource. Seek guidance from your manager and Human Resources for the most expeditious way to handle this case and minimize your investment.

Box 4: Willing, Unable

If you are going to have a people problem, this is a great category for it. I have long counseled managers that it is better to have a person where you occasionally have to throw some water on the flames versus always carrying a match to get them going. We'll assume this willing person is lit and ready to burn, but needs some help.

Once you have identified the circumstance where help is needed, you are ready to engage. Again, the perspective needs to be on the behavior, not the person.

- "I noticed there were errors in the sales analysis report today. Let's talk about how it is put together and make sure the spreadsheet is working properly."

This is a situation that may require training – perhaps brief informal instruction on a process step or maybe more formal instruction around technical knowledge. It may also be an issue that can be managed with coaching rather than training. If a person lacks confidence or needs subtle suggestions when practicing a skill, he is a candidate for coaching. Training is particularly suited to circumstances where there is a knowledge deficit.

If you feel it's a training issue, the nature of the problem coupled with the makeup of your team and your own capability will determine whether it makes sense for you to be involved versus a team member. Keep in mind that this can be a development opportunity for somebody on your team to mentor a peer that needs help, especially if it involves domain expertise that a more senior person can share. If it is a quick and simple problem and you are knowledgeable regarding the solution, or if coaching is required, you should handle it.

Like Box 3, this may also be a case where an individual is misplaced so be certain to make a thoughtful assessment as to whether you believe the individual is suited to the work in question. The time and money you can invest in correcting the ability issue will vary from organization to organization, and smaller firms and small teams may have little leeway to accommodate a team member who cannot produce. It is particularly easy to over-invest in this situation where somebody is willing but unable. Unlike Box 3, however, this may be a resource that is worthy of reassignment where an appropriate placement is available and the ability issue can't be overcome.

Coaching Explained

You probably can't remember the first time you heard this term. If you have ever participated in an organized sports activity you no doubt had a coach who not only called the shots, but also provided guidance and tips on technique, rules and strategy. In a business setting it's really no different. When somebody is undertaking a task, they may need some subtle course corrections, or coaching. As used here we intend this term to cover those short, brief instructional asides that you provide to your charges, usually with a positive connotation. Quick, simple bits of guidance that happen in the normal course of events are powerful tools to reinforce or encourage behavior.

- "This spreadsheet looks pretty good, but try sorting the data by date before you send it out. The managers may want to see the changes over time."

Counseling, as used here, is more of a two-way dialog meant to explore thoughts or feelings behind behavior. You need to talk about the underlying motives in an active, two-way discussion because you can't see them. A counseling interaction is not necessarily negative or corrective, but it assumes a more drawn out interaction than coaching.

Timing, Timing, Timing

Realtors always think in terms of location, but leaders rely on timing. Correcting problem behavior with team members is most effective when the feedback occurs as close to the incident as is practical. When you notice an exception relative to the behavioral expectations that have been established you must act quickly. Delaying intervention has the effect of condoning the inappropriate behavior and increases the difficulty level for correcting it later. Hesitating to act has the added impact of making a withdrawal from your credibility account. If you suspect problem behavior you must also act quickly – in this case it means putting yourself in a position to confirm or dispel your suspicion. The better alternative is to draw on your own observation for corrective feedback, but you may ultimately have to rely on input from others such as a fellow manager or a team member. In those cases be especially diligent in gathering and assessing input so you have confidence in addressing the concern. Finally, you should not call somebody out in front of other team members so if you have to briefly delay your intervention to manage the setting of your discussion that's the preferred course of action.

Guidelines for Conducting A Feedback Discussion

Here is a model for conducting the corrective feedback discussion. Having a path for this discussion is key to approaching the situation with confidence, and this model will serve you in a variety of circumstances where you will be giving feedback. Most of the time you will have brief "drive by" interactions that last a couple minutes but at the other extreme you will have serious sit downs where a job may be at stake. In either case – and everything in between - the following provides a framework for you to effectively deliver the feedback.

- **Focus on the behavior, not the person.** There are books galore on this point alone – it is the BEHAVIOR you are concerned with, not the person. Granted the two are inextricably connected, but your approach to addressing the issue should never feel like a personal attack. Remember – your goal is to change the behavior to correct the problem not to punish the person.
  - o "I want to talk to you about the way in which you responded to Tom in today's design review meeting."

- **YOU may need a few minutes to cool down** before you confront the person about the behavior. If it is something that really got you steamed you must be able to calmly discuss it.

- **Get your thoughts together before you start.** You want to get your point across in a concise way, and be confident you can clearly articulate your response to what behavior has to stop, start or change. As support for your case, you need to identify the business implications for not making the correction. These may be implications for the individual, team, customers or organization. You should be able to state the business implications distinctly from any personal consequences that may be on the table. You can cover both in this discussion, but the reason for the corrective feedback is primarily the business implication.
  - o "Your responses to Tom's ideas have a dismissive tone to them that causes him hold back his thoughts. I'm concerned that it has a similar effect on other team members and ultimately stifles the creative flow of ideas."

- **Identify a timeline.** You should expect immediate and permanent conformance to certain expectations such as not fighting or eliminating harassment. Repeat offenses are grounds for termination in those cases. If it is a capability or training issue, more time may be required, along with specific support from you to make sure the training takes place and "takes". Your manger or an HR representative can give you some guidance on what the practice has been for handling these issues within your organization. One of my favorite sayings is that treating two people exactly the same is the least fair thing you can do. Although no two cases are exactly alike, maintaining a semblance of consistency with past practice is important.

o "I expect you to find more productive ways to offer your critical comments, and you should never again respond to suggestions from other team members in a personal manner." OR

o "We'll monitor your data entry accuracy over the next sixty days to see if it comes up to the standard. We'll discuss your results at the end of each week so we both know if you are making progress."

- **Offer to help.** While the onus to change is on the associate, your job is to create conditions that are highly influential to assure the change happens. There is not much you can do to help somebody that is fighting or stealing, but when it comes to personal or skill development you should be a resource and a coach. A straightforward question is the best approach for this.

    o "Is there something I can do to help you find more effective ways to share your thoughts?"

- **Get the subject's commitment to the need for change, the timing and the plan** (if one was presented). It's critical that there is clarity about your expectations going forward. Again, direct questions are the preferred means for this.

    o "Do you have any questions about what we have discussed and are you going to be able to do what I am asking of you?"

- **Briefly recap the discussion and close.** Summarize the event in such a way that connotes your positive expectations for the requested change, and that this is not a personal issue. Your associate should leave feeling that you still have positive regard for him and the contribution he makes.

    o "I was concerned that your dismissive responses to Tom had the effect of stifling input from him and others. We agreed that you would work on managing your immediate reactions and be more thoughtful and sensitive in your responses. We also agreed that this change will happen immediately. I'll offer encouragement as I note your progress, and I look forward to more robust design review meetings going forward."

If there is a singular subject on the table this discussion should not last more than fifteen minutes. The time frame may vary up or down depending on the severity of the issue, but the prevailing wisdom here is that YOU own the meeting, YOU manage the content, and YOU create the closure.

Keeping the Discussion on Track

There are a few classic responses to corrective feedback for which you can be prepared. We will review a few of the most common, and identify techniques you can use to keep the discussion on track.

- **Arguing**. This is the most challenging participant you can expect in a feedback discussion. The responses generally fall into two categories. First, endless questions that are seemingly oriented toward clarification but only create a protracted discussion that prevents you from closing on the issue. The other is a debate over the details, particularly subjective factors. As a new leader these tactics are the most difficult because of the underlying lack of recognition for your authority – they are right and you obviously don't know what you are talking about otherwise they wouldn't have to set you straight with all the questions. There are two approaches I have found successful with these cases. I feel the stronger is to call them on the questions - something like "I feel you are asking me all these questions as a way of diverting us from completing the business at hand" or "These questions seem to be boring into details that distract us from the matter we came here to discuss." You can close the window of debate with this kind of response. For the craftiest argumentative types you may have to repeat this course correction before they get the idea of who is running this discussion. Even if it comes to that, your tone should always continue to be even and professional, but firm.

  Another approach is to tell them straight away that their method of debating the details isn't providing enlightenment to the message you are trying to deliver, and ask that they hold their questions until you have finished what you have to say. This should be reserved for the most strident arguers as it conveys a sense of "sit down and shut up" that can set an unconstructive tone. That said, it might be the best tool for the most challenging situations.

  Two final notes about giving corrective feedback to arguers. You should always make sure you provide an opportunity for the other person to ask questions, but you will have to use your judgment as whether or not your associate is turning things into a free for all that necessitates one of these tactics in return. Second, all of this assumes that you have your facts and figures squared away to the extent they will withstand scrutiny so you can be confident in truncating the argument cycle.

- **Crying**. Be prepared because it's going to happen. It is not a function of whether or not you are nice enough or sensitive enough. It may also come outside the corrective feedback scenario, but as a leader you will have to manage emotional behavior while interacting with your charges. Let's go over some mechanics you should have squared away before we get into managing the discussion. First, always be prepared with a box of tissues near your guest chairs or your desk. If you have an office try not to have the guest chairs facing the doorway or internal window. You don't want an emotional visitor having to worry about being on display in addition to breaking down in front of their boss. Finally, if you have a cube and you are planning a discussion that has the potential to elicit an emotional reaction (or any corrective or coaching discussion for that matter) arrange to have the discussion in a conference room or borrow an office.

  When it comes to managing a setting where your subject is crying there is one simple approach: don't directly acknowledge it and keep moving ahead. This doesn't mean you will respond insensitively to it. On the contrary – offer a tissue and give him a minute to compose himself as needed. Do not say something like "I understand that this may be upsetting to you – I'd be upset too" or "I can see that this is making you upset." In my book those responses are akin to "this is going to hurt." One caveat – it is highly likely the emotional responder will say something like "'I'm sorry for crying" which begs for a response. Keep it short, sweet and genuine with something like "I understand" or "that's OK" or "don't worry about it." Pause and support as needed, especially when the person is so distraught they aren't able to focus on the message or engage in the dialog, but keep things moving as best you can. Engaging him in what he should be doing going forward may be the best tonic for his emotional reaction. One final suggestion – if there are still residuals of the emotion when you are wrapped up (tears, red eyes, runny nose, etc.) you should offer to exit first and let him have the room to himself until he feels composed enough to go back in public.

- **Not engaging**. What do you do if you get through the entire corrective feedback discussion and you have yet to elicit a response from your associate? Ask them for one! If it hasn't already come up in your meeting, you should say something like "Say something!" OK maybe not those exact words, but if you encounter "a disconnector" you first have to determine if that kind of behavior is a symptom of why they are being corrected. If it is somebody who does not engage with their peers, participate in meetings, has poor verbal communication skills, etc. then that person is probably not the case we are referring to here. This is more about the one who, at the end of the meeting when you ask if they are able to make the change(s) you have asked for, just shrugs. One option is to repeat the question and perhaps they will get the hint and actually give you a response you can work with. This usually gets the easy cases to crack.

    For the harder cases, if they have not given you a response after the second attempt, try, "Are you willing to do what I asked?" This is a very assertive rebuff to a non-engagement type and the directness in the change of questioning will not be lost on them. If you are still not getting a commitment from them, they are a candidate for discharge. You have far too many ways in which you can invest your valuable time than to play games with somebody who chooses not to engage. As mentioned earlier in this chapter you should ALWAYS seek direction from your manager and human resources before you have a corrective feedback discussion so you are not only squared away on your documentation, but also so you know how much latitude you have to close out a difficult discussion like this. If you really want to push the envelope with your HR people, suggest to them that the person has, in effect resigned, as he is not willing to perform the work requested. Terminating somebody under the auspices of a resignation makes it a voluntary separation and will probably get you out of providing unemployment if you choose to contest it. If HR doesn't support the voluntary resignation concept, tell them you want to let the individual go for insubordination

Let me repeat: YOU own this conversation, YOU are the master of this environment, and YOU will manage the process. Have some confidence. There will be times that your subject will argue, cry, deflect or not engage, but that doesn't mean you can't have a productive meeting.

"You Want This In the Arm or In the Buttocks?"

Think about the approach used in hospitals and clinics when the staff has to give somebody a shot or draw blood, or administer a test that involves something invasive. I doubt you ever had a doctor or nurse kick things off by saying "this is going to hurt" accompanied by a pained facial expression and body language that suggested fingernails on the blackboard. But that may seem eerily similar to how a boss has given you feedback in the past. Nobody enjoys making another human being uncomfortable or ill at ease yet it's a common, albeit unintentional, result of many leaders' approach to giving feedback.

The approach you should use in giving feedback is similar to the clinical model of preparing people for procedures: very matter of fact, with level and confident vocal pitch, and with direct eye contact. If you expect to avoid telegraphing the "this is going to hurt" signal you have to believe it will not hurt either of you. Granted, the nurse that gave you the shot has done it many times, knows how to handle myriad reactions, is very familiar with the tools used, and cleverly uses distraction to keep you from tensing up. I can guarantee you the first few people that got shots from that nurse were not the most comfortable recipients. The most recent patients thought they were in the hands of a master.

You can't expect to handle feedback at the master level right off the bat, but a big part of being effective in giving feedback is your body language, voice and your facial expressions. You should view the opportunity to give feedback as a vital tool in assuring you get the most out of your team, and relish these interactions versus dread them. Being well prepared for this discussion will help, but as with most things, practice makes perfect.

How Do I Display Self-Confidence When I am Shaking in My Boots?

As mentioned earlier, confidence comes with experience and you only get the experience if you make a practice of giving feedback. I know, it sounds like a circular discussion, but we hope you appreciate the underlying logic. You now have a model to guide your interaction when giving feedback, and we'll throw in a few tips that will add to your confidence and hopefully predispose you to act.

- Go into the situation with the belief that the person will be willing to meet your request. This doesn't mean you expect they will be happy about having the discussion, but they WILL want to get past the problem, even if it means they have to change something they are doing.

- Be prepared. You now have insight into how frame the discussion and some techniques for managing challenging individuals, so use those tools.

- Do this often. There are plenty of opportunities – large and small – to have a word with somebody on your team, so use them to your advantage and start practicing this skill and building your bank of experience.

- Solicit feedback on your feedback skills. Sometimes the simplest, most obvious tactics can be extremely powerful but are easily overlooked. When your team members understand you are "a work in progress" it will reduce the heat you put on yourself to be perfect. More importantly, you will get input that can help you improve your skills. As I said, feedback is a circle!

It's Great to be Positive

The primary focus for this chapter is the more challenging corrective discussion, but don't lose sight of the value of positive feedback, which is often referred to as recognition. Behavioral research tells us that the most powerful way of shaping behavior or making sure a given behavior is demonstrated again is to reinforce it. Rather than the pellets given to rodents in the lab's maze, you have praise and thanks at your disposal. The best part is they are both free!

The most challenging aspect of positive reinforcement, or recognition, is recognizing the situation where you can give it. Seriously. So much of a leader's time is focused on issues of non-conformity such as process and deliverable problems that have to be addressed, and that preoccupation can blind you to the abundance of things that conform. There is a training program and video that was produced a number of years ago that sheds light on this in a creative way. The case is centered on a supervisor in a machine shop name Sid and is called *The Sid Story* (Coastal Training Technologies, Corp.) Who said training people aren't creative?

Sid often comes home at the end of his day to find his son's bike in the driveway causing him to get out of the car, move the bike, pull his car into the garage and scold his son. Sid's revelation comes from his son asking him why he always notices one thing he doesn't do correctly but never seems to notice the things he does get right, like making his bed. Sid takes this new insight to his job where he makes a point of identifying something that does conform to his expectations and passing along a compliment accordingly. Sid doesn't make a national holiday of this – he just briefly acknowledges the behavior when he sees it and moves on. The recognition only happens with a conscious effort on Sid's part to be on the lookout for something worthy of acknowledgement. He calls it planned spontaneous recognition. The story goes on to document how his crew becomes a high-performing unit at the shop, with that success attributable, in part, to Sid's approach to recognizing his team members. There are three keys to Sid's method:

- Quick and dirty
- Identify a specific behavior or result to acknowledge
- Frequent enough that it becomes a routine but still seems genuine

Epilogue

Many times during your day you will be faced with the task of doing the right thing versus the expedient thing. The underlying assumption is the right thing is more difficult, or, at the very least, less fun. This is typically how people view corrective feedback. Great leaders, however, unflinchingly maintain the right path. If you have resolved to establish and maintain credibility as a leader, you have to be honest. In Chapter 5, the third item on Art's list of credibility builders is unimpeachable honesty, and you will develop a reputation for being honest if your people can always count on you to give them candid feedback that includes suggestions for improvement as well as recognition. Withholding feedback undermines your perceived honesty and marginalizes the potential contribution at the individual level, the team level and for the organization as a whole. There's that feedback circle again.

Commit yourself to ALWAYS being direct and honest with you team members regarding their performance and behavior. And in spite of Mark Twain's advice to the contrary, you always need to do the right thing!

> "Well, then says I' what's the use in learning to do the right thing when it's troublesome to do right and ain't no trouble to do wrong, and the wages are the same?"
> -Huckleberry Finn by Mark Twain.

Discussion Questions: Sharon's Team Could Do No Wrong and Alan Discovers Karma

- *What 'Box' would you place Julie and Alan in? Why?*
- *What is Pat's next step with Julie?*
- *Should Fred give Alan another chance?*
- *What performance and behavior objectives would you design for Julie and Alan?*

For ideas on how the authors view the situation at Apex and the issues outlined above, visit the Leadership Resource Center at www.management-innovations. com, and click on Practical Lessons-Discussion Questions.

PREFACE TO CHAPTER 10

Finding Talent in Unusual Places

Mark sat in the waiting area of Arogent Communications waiting for the representative to help him out. He hated coming to these stores because he knew that he was in for a run-around. The formula was consistent: confusing plans and lengthy contract commitments delivered by disinterested clerks. He hardly had time for this, as he had a list of things to work on a mile long, including meeting with HR to figure out a recruiting plan for his open positions. It was hard to run a telemarketing team without good help, and Mark had lost a number of team members during his first few months.

After a few minutes of daydreaming about his problems, Mark noticed something unusual going on in the store. There were four clerks working with customers, with one of the clerks, a young man, seemingly functioning as the go-to person for the others. He was handling his customers with a smile and an air of efficiency, listening to their concerns and offering solutions to their issues. His approach had a visible impact on the customers, and they seemed to relax once they felt like their needs were being met. Even more amazing, at the same time that he was serving customers, he was being peppered by questions from his associates, and he deftly answered their concerns, without interrupting his own customer service. Amazingly, problems were being solved, new contracts being signed and people walking out the door with new cell phones and smiles on their faces.

"Sure wish I had a few like him," thought Mark as he waited for his turn.

You Can Lead A Horse to Water

Susan took her responsibility to support the professional development of her teammates seriously. Although she was a first-time manager in the middle of her first year, she had received positive feedback on her performance so far from her manager, and she sensed that her team members appreciated her efforts on their behalf. However, one team member, John Kachena, the lead for the second shift help desk, not only had resisted her efforts to get him to talk about his future objectives, but he was refusing to sit down and complete Apex's Career Plan/Profile document. His response to her inquiries left her uncertain of what to do. The last time she tried to approach him about this topic, he responded with the following:

"Susan, why do you and Apex insist on knowing my future plans. I come in every day and do my job and according to my past few reviews, I do it very well. But this insistence on getting me to sit down and talk about what I want to do with my life makes no sense. Frankly, it's none of your or anyone else's business." Susan was speechless as John finished talking and abruptly turned around and left her office.

CHAPTER 10
CHIEF TALENT SCOUT AND DEVELOPER

There is a new buzzword winging its way through the business world. You can't go to a conference, attend a big meeting or get through a cocktail party without hearing the term 'C-level'. For a long time we have heard about CEOs, CFOs and COOs; in recent times we have ginned up CTO (Chief Technical Officer), CIO (Chief Information Officer), CMO (Chief Marketing Officer) and, in deference to the age of Sarbanes-Oxley, we now have CCOs (Chief Compliance Officer). Everybody at the top of the organizational food chain is a chief something or other – we just have to hope there are still some tribe members around to be Chief of. Even as a new or near term leader you have an opportunity for a C title: Chief Talent Scout. We'll also assume you will take an active role in developing the talent you find.

Every organization I have ever been a part of has had a chief talent scout and developer. And typically everybody knows who it is. Truly great firms will have several, but there is always one "alpha scout" who leads the pack in this area. It's the woman or man people want to work for, and they see an association with that person as a pre-greased path to bigger and better opportunities. Too often the association with the scout/developer and subsequent roles their charges enjoy may be viewed as kismet, but doesn't the virtuoso make playing her instrument seem effortless? I can assure you that in both cases success is not coincidental. Over time, the scout/developer's methods evolve from scrounging and turning over rocks looking for talent, to the point where talented resources will begin to gravitate to him or her. Who wouldn't want this reputation in their portfolio? If you do, read on. If not, pass this book on to somebody else who may find this information useful.

The Pride Factor

My partner will wax at length about the joy he gets from seeing people develop and grow. Not because he is a trained marketing assassin with extraordinary communication skills, but because it truly moves him. You expect that sort of thing from human resources people, but others? Not so much. Along with getting things done and moving an organization forward, seeing individuals prosper is the best reward a leader has. Our research participants universally reported that contributing to the success of others is the best part of their job. This was reported in a variety of ways:

- "It's great to see others grow and evolve."
- "My biggest thrill is seeing people enjoy their work"
- "I get a sense of fulfillment creating opportunities for deserving team members."
- "I know I have done my job right when other managers want my people. It doesn't get any better than that!"
- "The most rewarding part for me is the opportunity to coach and mentor others."
- "My sense of accomplishment comes from the career advancement of my direct reports."
- "I like my job most when I can teach others what I have learned and notice they avoid some of the pitfalls I encountered."
- "My biggest rush comes when somebody achieves his or her goals, especially ones they thought were beyond their grasp."

The feeling of pride you get parallels raising kids. Unless you have had the opportunity to be the one letting go of the back of the seat of a bicycle with recently removed training wheels, you may not fully appreciate this. I sum it up by suggesting that the connection you have to those whom you select and promote is like no other you will have with a non-relative.

The Story of a Successful Shepherd

My first job in human resources was at a manufacturing facility. I was hired to replace a guy who had the same educational background and went to the same school I did. His promotion created the opening for me. In getting to know my department manager I found out that he had been around the block a great deal before settling in at the location where I was hired. He had over twenty-five years with the company, and had been part of the start-up team for three plants prior to coming to this location to help with its start-up. This was a sizable organization in total – over 10,000 people and nearly twenty manufacturing locations - but as I gained experience, the company-wide circle seemed to get smaller in a few very intriguing ways. First, I came across names of human resources management types from other locations on various forms in employee files at my location. Second, the company had "All-HR" meetings every other year or so, which presented the opportunity to meet the people behind the signatures and hear about their experiences at my location. I heard them reflect positively on the time they spent there, which made me realize that at some point they all worked for the same guy that I reported to right now. At this point in time there were more people in the overall human resources management team of this company that had worked for him, than had not. I and one other associate who started a couple years after I did were the end of the line however, as we were part of his team when he retired. Although I moved on to a different entity, I recently reconnected with that last hire and she is currently a vice president with that same organization. What a great legacy.

I can tell you that it was a number of years into my career before the meaningfulness of this circle truly dawned on me. I can also tell you I still use some of the same parables and methods for getting a point across without being directive that he did, and I know that it is one of the traits that people who have worked for me through the years have valued. God bless you, Glenn.

Scout School is in Session

I can write about how I scout talent, and Art can tell you what he does, but much like professional wrestlers, you should develop your own methods for where, when and how to find talent. I'll let you in on a little secret early in this chapter – the where and when questions have the easiest answers: always and everywhere. The how question is a bit more involved. Let's explore how you can go about becoming a legend.

Art and I worked with a sales manager who was a voracious scout. This person was always on the lookout for talent to fill the stable – whether it was for his team or a peer's team, he was always looking for good people. It was a mindset for this person. I would often hear about the people he met when he recounted a recent trip to a seminar or conference, with as much or more passion of the subject matter of the event he attended. Further, he made a point of scheduling at least one "get to know you" meeting each month with a new contact. You can find books galore on networking and expanding your base of contacts, and in some ways this is very similar behavior. The primary difference between networking and scouting is that in networking you don't often know how a potential relationship will ultimately benefit either party. In this context as talent scout we are describing predatory behavior – you know exactly what you are looking for and you want all the good players on your bench or waiting to join your organization. Period. Not everybody you will meet is going to be a keeper, but if you aren't getting your line in the water on a regular basis you can't expect to be a very good fisherman, much less a guide or a scout.

So how did the organization benefit from this sales manager's scouting activity? First and foremost, we usually had a shorter turn-around cycle when an opening occurred in his region. There was an added benefit in the fact that he was not stingy – if he had a contact that could meet the needs of a part of the organization other than his own he didn't have to be asked. Additionally, there was enough confidence in the screening activity that had already taken place that the process for evaluating candidates could also be reduced. Sometimes this manager would invite contacts to the office to meet key people as a way of getting the organization's hooks into the person in the event there were no immediate needs, giving our company a chance to get personally entrenched with the contact ahead of another organization.

Getting Started

We have described scouting activity as an art form in the example of the sales manager. Be assured that there are plenty of basic tactics, however, that will serve you well. As with any routine, with enough use it becomes second nature and your execution will become as smooth as glass. Here are some tactics to get you started.

1. Express interest in others. You may have to do some digging to find the gold, and appearances can be deceiving. Cliché's aside,

don't discount somebody's potential value without scratching below the surface.

2. Think "fit" at all times. HOW can this resource be deployed for the best results? Are they being used to their potential? Not everybody is cut out to be a leader or company president, but there is plenty of work to do in any firm, and success is largely a function of having the right resources in the right roles at the right time.

3. ALWAYS be on the lookout. Always. Did you meet somebody at the gas station that piqued your interest? The grocery store? Something about the way she looked you in the eye when you dealt with her? Work-related interactions with others are obvious choices, but don't discount the people you meet in your everyday life.

4. Encourage others to be on the lookout. This can include family and friends as well as work colleagues. If others know what you look for in people and that you are always willing to at least meet or talk with someone you will broaden your reach considerably.

5. Share the wealth. If you can't use somebody that impressed you but feel they can be valuable to somebody else – even if it is another organization – make the referral. You know the cliché that applies here – what goes around comes around.

6. Maintain your integrity. Don't make promises on which you cannot deliver. If you tell somebody you will call, then do it. If you say you will pass along information to somebody else, do it. Then follow up with a note letting them know you didn't forget about them and you completed the commitment. Further, if you don't see a fit for somebody tell the truth. You will be more embarrassed and frustrated in the long run if the person tries to reconnect because you used a lame excuse like "nothing now, but maybe in a couple months." More importantly, giving somebody an honest assessment may provide the motivation to pursue development that will improve their chances of pursing a given path.

7. Keep it simple. When you initially talk to somebody about their career aspirations, don't feel that you have to get their unabridged life story. See if what they say in a brief interaction aligns with your initial perception. If it does, it is probably worth a deeper investment. If not, politely move on.

8. Resist the "just like me" approach. A common pitfall when people are new to the screening process is that they demonstrate a preference or positive assessment for people who they perceive to be similar to themselves. This may not be all bad if you are likable and erudite like Art, but if you are irascible and ill mannered like me you need a more effective yardstick. See number 9.

9. Get some training. Duh! One of the things we hope you take away from this book is a belief that you expect to learn continuously through your life (not just your working life, either). Get acquainted with behavioral interviewing methods if you are not already, and get involved in screening candidates even if it does not involve an opening for your team. You can use those experiences to refine your skills and get real world practice evaluating talent. The opportunity to compare notes with others as you take part in the screening and evaluation process is a huge learning experience that you cannot buy on the open market. Take advantage of it!

As you can see there are many dimensions to being a talent scout. Use your creativity to make this important task an enjoyable one that fits comfortably into your normal course of business. Most importantly, scout everywhere and scout often.

Scout AND Developer?

Here's a provocative question for you – do you suppose it is possible to be a good scout and not be a good developer? I suppose it is in the realm of possibility, but I think there is a strong positive correlation between the skills for scouting and developing that suggests the two go together. They both start with a genuine interest in people. I don't believe you can genuinely source talent and let it lie fallow. If you can let yourself do that to another human being, you should choose another line of work. Something that doesn't involve working with people at all...perhaps stuffing envelopes at home.

I think you can definitely be better at one versus the other. You would probably find that those in the highest-level jobs in large organizations begin to cultivate and rely upon alliances with trusted members of their staff (the venerable right arm) and look for people suited to that role. The gold for leaders near the top tends to lie more in identifying talented individuals who may have already been developed to a high-performing level - and giving them challenging work - than in developing them. I believe this seemingly narrow leader behavior is just about expediency - a function of that kind of work and the time pressure faced in those roles. As a new leader, however, you should develop balanced skills in both areas – scouting AND developing because it will serve you well in your job AND because it is the right thing to do.

Maybe we should take a minute – or should I say a couple sentences – to describe what we mean by developing others. I have used the metaphor "bigger, faster, stronger" in describing or asking about the difference in an individual's capabilities today versus a year ago. To the extent you can describe the person with a positive term that ends in "er" you can consider development to have taken place. There is a bit of art in identifying development activities that match the individual or organization's needs, but if you find any means to help somebody work towards their potential, you are on the right track. I think the U.S. Army commercial said it best with their slogan, "Be all you can be."

This may be starting to sound like hyperbole so let's move on to something more tangible. You will find the following guidelines useful in establishing development plans for your charges.

Four Axioms of Developing Others

1. You can't do it FOR them. Ultimately, each of us owns responsibility for our own development, but you are responsible for setting the stage and removing organizational – and perhaps personal or motivational – impediments to development for the people who report to you. Remember – you can't do their work, but you can help make the process of completing their tasks more efficient.

2. You can't do it TO them. As a leader you can demonstrate motivation and excitement for life-long learning, enthusiastically and publicly promoting the opportunity to apply your new skills or knowledge. This will translate into healthy buy-in from others.

3. It must be useful. In other words, if the outcome isn't something that can be applied don't waste the time or money. Development doesn't have to be limited to on-the-job constructs – think more broadly about the topic and developing the whole person. Odds are the person who is constantly overwhelmed at work probably has a time management issue at home as well. People with a healthy work and personal life balance will be more effective persons overall, not just at work.

4. Feedback is <u>critical</u> to the process. Consider everything from encouragement for undertaking and/or completing recommended activities to sharing observations of changes in behavior or results that you see.

One cautionary note – your focus in developing others is to leverage their strengths first and foremost. Secondarily, you want to minimize shortcomings or risk factors. DO NOT try to put the proverbial round pegs in square holes. We use a public speaking example several times in this book. If you have a reluctant speaker, you should provide low risk, coaching opportunities for her to practice addressing a group because that is a very necessary basic skill in today's knowledge economy. Do not over-invest your energy or hers in trying to make her a keynote speaker. Find a means to deploy people correctly, challenge them to build their skills, and get out of the way.

A Tool for Developing Others

For all of your important objectives you have to have a plan, and developing others is no exception. The following is an outline for a basic Individual Development Plan (IDP). In many organizations a component of the annual review may be dedicated to personal and professional development and it may very well cover the same topics you see below. We'll provide a brief overview of what should go in each section so you can make the most of your development planning efforts.

A working document template, and a sample completed document, can be found in the Manager's Toolkit at www.management-innovations.com along with further insights on IDPs and succession planning.

INDIVIDUAL DEVELOPMENT PLAN WORKSHEET

Employee_____ Manager_____

Date_____

CAREER PATH

Summarize this person's desired career path and compensation objectives. May be based on type of work as much as job title.

BUSINESS/INDUSTRY KNOWLEDGE

List specific aspects of the business or industry to learn that will benefit this person:

What action do you recommend taking on the above in the next 12 months? In what time frame?

What results are expected?

Will this result benefit current role or future roles or both? How?

Who is responsible for initiating action on the above?

PROFESSIONAL AND PERSONAL DEVELOPMENT

Identify specific professional development or training that will benefit this person. Consider domain expertise, compliance or regulatory knowledge, technical skills, and personal skills such as teamwork, time management, communication skills, etc.

What action do you recommend taking on the above in the next 12 months? In what time frame?

What results are expected?

Will this result benefit current role or future roles or both? How?

Who is responsible for initiating action on the above?

JOB/PROJECT ASSIGNMENTS

Identify on-the-job assignments to support BUSINESS/INDUSTRY KNOWLEDGE and/or PROFESSIONAL AND PERSONAL DEVELOPMENT.

What action do you recommend taking on the above in the next 12 months? In what time frame?

What results are expected?

Will this result benefit current role or future roles or both? How?

Who is responsible for initiating action on the above?

Now, let's go through the process for completing this form.

Career Path

Your first step is to gather data in two key areas. This data gathering can be done in one conversation, but if you have that conversation on more than one occasion over a period of time both parties will be better satisfied with the results. This data gathering should be viewed as an iterative, two-party process. You can't expect to cook up the plan independently, present it, and get strong buy-in. Further, if you work on it together over time you are likely to have a richer product in the end – one that reflects your combined creative thinking efforts. These interactions also present a golden opportunity for you to model the enthusiasm you have for this aspect of your leadership role. Filling in the form is a mechanical task, but developing the content is the provocative part – don't shortchange this step.

A few additional thoughts on career path involve the direction of the path and timing. Some people will know just where they want to go and when, but many will not. Not all careers are defined by vertical movement, and many times the means to keep people challenged and engaged is to move them laterally not just up. If a young associate only has designs for a few years down the road don't feel you should press them for a long-term plan. A long-tenured but competent associate may be very content in their role and may only need development sufficient to keep them current in their role. Don't hold anybody back, but don't limit your thinking that only upward movement is commendable or appropriate in all cases.

Finally, compensation is a powerful topic relative to career planning. As we mentioned in Chapter 2 this is a vital step, but discussing compensation should happen AFTER you talk about the work they want to do. You should be knowledgeable of the implications of different careers. Technicians make more than administrative assistants, and sales people make more money than everybody.

Business/Industry Knowledge

It is not appropriate or practical for each associate in the firm to know virtually everything about the business, but there is operational knowledge that will be beneficial based on their current and/ or expected roles. In general, we suggest that all associates have at least a conceptual understanding of your business including the products/services offered, the market space in which it competes, and an understanding of your primary competitors. Further, you should assure that the associate has a solid understanding about the business processes just prior and following their function. Do they handle something that comes from another internal department or from somebody else on their team? Where does their work go when it's complete? Having insight into the operations surrounding their function will be a huge benefit when you try to engage them in innovation.

The following items are common to the last three sections of the IDP:

- The "action" question is just what it says – identify the activity that you expect to take place. Focus on action during the next 12 months – longer-term items should go on next year's plan.

- Now we get to the heart of your writing work - results. It is typically easier to put the action to be taken into words than the outcome. Once you do, however, you will greatly increase the likelihood of successfully meeting the objective, largely because the expectation and rationale are clear.

- Another simple question – you are going to identify the action as a current or future benefit, and how (not why) with as much specificity as possible.

- There may often be a shared ownership for a development activity. The leader may have to get the expense approved, arrange coverage, etc. Where projects are involved, that may be the sole responsibility of the associate. These factors are about making the development activity happen, but keep in mind that the associate owns the expected outcome such as demonstrating a new or improved capability.

Professional and Personal Development

This section is intended to cover subject matter related to their profession. If the associate is an accountant, is she they fluent with the report writing package in your accounting system? Has she stayed current in the latest compliance requirements? This is where you will address items needed to keep the team member employable independent of their current job. You may have read about the evolved social contract between employers and employees. It used to be the employer was accountable for <u>employment</u> assuming the employee kept his nose clean (you have to wonder how that cliché started). The current evolution of the social contract holds that the employer should be accountable for making sure the employee is <u>employable</u> in the world at large because a given employer can't commit to permanent employment. Keeping people current in their professional skills goes a long way in supporting the commitment of employability.

Personal development covers skills independent of domain expertise, but pertinent to executing the job. You might think of them as skills related to how they do things as opposed to what they are doing. Things such as time management, written communication and teamwork can go in this section. Don't succumb to thinking that these skills aren't critical to somebody's job. We guarantee that at least half of the performance issues you are going to deal with will involve behavior beyond job knowledge or technical skills. Capturing those concerns here in the form of a development opportunity can be an important step toward influencing a change of behavior, and in the worst case scenario, the foundation of a written warning later on.

Job/Project Assignments

The most powerful section of this form is Job and Project Assignments. Research shows that the most profound development experiences that people have throughout their careers occur on-the-job. These assignments are pure gold for you as a leader – there is typically no out of pocket expense and they are bound only by your creativity. Is there an opportunity for a short term job swap or interim job shadowing experience that can marry up with components of a career plan? Does anybody *really* know what goes on in shipping and why it takes two days for orders to leave the building once you complete the paperwork? Is there an opportunity to collaborate on something with another functional area of the organization? Is it appropriate to give a live reporting assignment to somebody who is terrified of public speaking? Aside from the potential visibility, I'm betting the best public speaker on your team doesn't have as much to gain from the experience. Relish every opportunity you have to use on the job development to enrich your team members and their capabilities.

Don't let dust accumulate on your IDPs. Even if they are embedded in your annual review process, you should revisit them regularly throughout the year. I'd suggest quarterly at a minimum, ideally once a month to make sure the plan is being followed. Having a monthly meeting with each of your charges is a great way to stay connected on everything from general expectations to project status to improvement needs to development plans. You'll be both surprised and disappointed at how many demands will otherwise clog up your calendar if you don't overtly stay on top of your IDPs, and the time required to do justice to the update will be less per occasion if you do it more often. As Art said earlier in the book, don't be a victim of the urgent and unimportant.

Epilogue

You have to ask yourself a couple questions at this point. Do you truly believe it is possible to find somebody out there who is more capable than you? Are you confident and secure enough to be willing to select or promote somebody who could end up being your boss? Chances are you will be the leader of somebody whose career outpaces yours, so you should be the kind of person who can take great pride in that fact. This will be much easier to do if you genuinely and meaningfully played a role in getting that woman or man on the road to whatever lies ahead of them.

Harvey Firestone, founder of tire and rubber manufacturing company that bears his name, once said "The growth and development of people is highest calling of leadership." If you want to develop into a great leader, you should continually be a student of successful people and how they got there. We guarantee that you will see that successful leaders regularly surrounded themselves with extremely capable people. Don't think that resulted from the chance to pick staff members from a preferred list. Also, take note of how competent people follow good leaders from one organization to the next. Can we agree that you would like to find yourself in that situation? You will need a solid team to deliver on your organization's objectives, and you ultimately play a significant role in developing their capabilities.

In the first 10 chapters we presented some very actionable tactics for you to get off to a great start as a leader. The question that follows is "now what?" Let's go on to a chapter that will challenge you to use the great team you have built to add value to the organization.

Discussion Questions for: Finding Talent in Unusual Places and You Can Lead a Horse to Water.

- *What would you do if you were Mark observing the performance of the representative in the Arogent Communications store?*
- *What's the talent scout lesson learned here?*
- *Why might John be uncomfortable about talking about his career plans?*
- *Is his reluctance a warning sign or something that should be respected.*
- *What would you do if you were Susan?*

For ideas on how the authors view the situation at Apex and the issues outlined above, visit the Leadership Resource Center at www.management-innovations. com, and click on Practical Lessons-Discussion Questions.

PART FOUR
TYING IT ALL TOGETHER TO DRIVE RESULTS

PREFACE TO CHAPTER 11

BEHOLD THE POWER OF TEAMWORK!

Sara Davis had a great problem. She was listing out ideas to reward her mid-market product team for their recent innovation efforts. What had started out as a slow and contentious process had turned into a great example of effective brainstorming and collaboration. The final outcome—a new product idea that leveraged existing technologies that could be packaged together at a market disrupting price-point, would be ready for customer testing in two months and for sale after another thirty days. And while this product would be a stop-gap until the new architecture was available late next year, it would contribute to the top line without adding significant cost or even straining the existing resources.

Sara smiled recalling the early arguments over what to do, if anything. The new architecture team refused to budge on their plans and resources, and rightly so. The new product would be the future of the mid-market group at Apex, and delays were not acceptable. But when Bob Hobson, the technical lead and cross-functional representative from the customer support team had suggested "Project Duct Tape," as it came to be known, the wheels began moving. Before long, the group had identified a way to pull the pieces together without disrupting current programs, and each of the areas had volunteered some part-time resources to make it happen. Sales and marketing were ecstatic to have a new offering to promote and sell, and launch plans were already underway.

The Tennis Match

The story in George O'Connell's vertical market group was much different than what he was hearing from mid-market. The vertical team had been through three rounds of brainstorming, and the best they could string together was 15-minutes without an argument. In spite of George's repeated references to Victoria Pyott's challenge to the company to innovate, George had not found away to gain agreement that they needed to do anything. As a result, every session ended up in an argument over whether they were really in a crisis to begin with.

If George was being honest, he could trace most of the resistance to doing anything to one character, Paul Escamp, a long-time Apex engineer and one of the most vocal and stubborn people that George had ever met. Paul leveraged his long history with the company and employee #7 designation to push his opinion. And whenever anyone attempted to challenge him, Paul was quick to put them in his place. Paul's nemesis in these meetings was June Post, a confident and aggressive product leader who felt strongly about the need to do something, and she had even proposed a few interesting ideas. Unfortunately, Paul would have nothing to do with her input and almost every session reduced to a tennis match between the two, with June throwing an idea over the net and Paul batting it back across. George was beginning to think he would have to excuse the two from the next meeting and see what the rest of the group had to say. He needed to do something.

CHAPTER 11
CREATING A CULTURE OF
INNOVATION WITH YOUR TEAM

Welcome to the part in the book where we challenge you to take everything that we have been talking about and tie it together in pursuit of doing great things with your team and for your firm. This chapter on building a culture of innovation and the next (In Pursuit of Operational Excellence) are intrinsically linked, and yet different enough to merit their own treatment. In the opinion of the authors, operationally excellent teams tend to have more characteristics of an innovative culture and innovative teams tend to be teams that have crossed the operational excellence bar and are hungry to find new ways to add value to their firm. Rather than debate the "chicken or egg" dilemma of which comes first, our approach is to encourage you to read these two as part and parcel of each other, and to remind you that the best results come from those teams that are confident enough to pursue their tasks with a spirit of innovation and experimentation.

You are Responsible for Creating a Culture with
Your Team that Encourages Innovation

In case no one told you that you are responsible for driving innovations that improve your firm's position in the market or the ability of your organization to serve internal and external customers and execute strategies, consider yourself so informed. Innovation in an organization is not the sole responsibility of engineers, programmers, any one department or even managers and top-level executives wearing creative titles. Driving innovation in programs, processes and approaches is the job of every manager, supervisor and ultimately every associate in the company. As a leader, it is a core responsibility that you carry, whether it is in your job description or not.

Most people equate innovation with a firm's ability to generate exciting new products and services that attract customers, grow sales and profitability and leave competitors reeling to formulate a response. While new products and services are the lifeblood of a firm's growth, you don't have to leave all of the fun to the engineers. In my own experience, I've marveled at a number of my teams as they produced new methods of marketing to and educating customers, identified new ways of bundling, pricing and financing products and created new programs to help motivate channel partners to carry more of our offerings products and displace our competitors. I've seen innovations in assessing territory potential and assigning quotas, unique methods of motivating and compensating sales teams and innovations in planning and choreographing internal and external meetings. I've watched as unique approaches in marketing, messaging and thought-leadership changed the face of a marketplace and forced competitors to flail in search of a response.

Innovation-A Lot of Talk but Not As Much Action

Given the red-hot popularity of the topic of innovation in the business press during the past few years, we expected to come out of the research phase for this book armed with insights and Ah Ha ideas about how leaders at all levels are driving innovation through and across their organizations. Imagine our surprise when an otherwise remarkable and committed group of respondents shrugged their shoulders and indicated in not so many words that they were more focused on hitting their targets and helping their team members and that innovation was reserved for occasional brainstorming or annual planning. Of course, there were the expected comments about empowering teams and individuals to improve or collaborating on goal setting, but otherwise, there were very few insights on best practices and approaches to driving innovation. It was our observation that in spite of the popularity of the topic, very few early career and mid-level leaders understand that this is a core part of their role, nor do they have the knowledge about the processes and approaches necessary to create a culture of innovation with their team. After the interviews, we attacked this content with a new vigor, and hope that this chapter serves as a good starting point for you to begin building your own innovation machine with your team.

Working with a team that is focused on identifying new ways to improve in all facets, including process, programs and approaches is remarkably fun and provides a huge boon to productivity and ultimately profitability for a firm. The opportunity to innovate is open to all teams and individuals regardless of function. As a leader of a team, you are responsible for creating a culture of innovation within your own domain and then feeding this innovation machine with support, reinforcement, reward, encouragement in the face of defeat and ultimately, a moon-shot mentality that has your team reaching far beyond the visible sky. Sound exciting? Of course it is, but first, let's tackle the fundamentals, and start with a working definition of innovation and some examples of great and creative teams at work in this domain.

A Digestible Definition of Innovation and More Examples:

Simply stated, the "innovation" that we are referencing in this chapter is about <u>creating incremental positive value for the firm by solving vexing problems with unique and reproducible approaches</u>. All pieces and parts in this definition have to be accounted for to be truly innovative.

The change or improvement has to create positive incremental value for the firm, most often expressed in terms of time or dollars, but also important measures like brand equity, share of mind and quality. To be innovative, we require the solution to address a vexing business problem, preferably one that translates ultimately into some form of customer value or competitive advantage. And finally, the solution should be capable of being institutionalized and reproduced so that the gain is permanent versus fleeting. Some great examples of where I have seen innovation improve a business's effectiveness include:

- A marketing communications team created a remarkably effective way to educate an untapped market on the challenges and solutions to complex data management problems, while increasing leads, brand recognition, market presence, sales and profitability. The team leveraged a new medium in web based education and promotion using new technology (voice over internet protocol) while establishing the firm as a thought-leader. Every time a competitor would follow (and they did), the team would add a "twist" to the approach, strengthening the interest and ultimately the reputation of the firm. The sales team didn't complain either as qualified leads increased exponentially and even the CFO was happy as cost per qualified lead decreased significantly.

- A technology supplier to a fast food franchise marketplace became the unrivaled market leader to this group by responding to quality problems with their equipment in a unique way. Faced with expulsion from the approved vendor's list, the technology provider owned up to the quality problems; proposed and delivered timely solutions and then invested in creating an advocacy group that went on to help the franchise community organize and solve many vexing business problems. The equipment provider ultimately facilitated the identification, prioritization and solution development of problems having nothing directly to do with their equipment, but everything to do with the value they wanted to offer as a problem solver and solutions provider in this community.

- A cross-functional team solved a market positioning dilemma for a new technology and in the process created their own unique process for message-mapping, which quickly became the standard for developing, refining and testing messages as well as training spokespeople on delivering a consistent message internally and externally. This smallest of market participants consistently received the highest rankings from market and technology analysts for market strategy and market messaging.

- A technology supplier to the life safety market shook up a sleepy industry by throwing convention out the window and introducing a number of new products that were suited for environments heretofore viewed as untenable for the accurate functioning of the equipment. While the products in and of themselves did not sell in huge quantities, they succeeded in creating a persona of innovation around this firm in a marketplace where no one had grabbed the mantle of leadership. The publicity and ultimately increased brand equity and recognition contributed to the growth of the firm's top line for years to come.

- The same Marketing team referenced earlier was challenged to out-promote their much larger competitors at industry tradeshows, albeit, with budgets that were a fraction of the size of those firms. They established a mantra of "own the show," to guide their planning for industry trade show events. This filter drove a tremendous number of experiments and ultimately innovations in the planning and delivery of industry events. The "own the show" theme resulted in programs and show-floor activities that created fits for competitors and were the source of tremendous fun not to mention improvement in leads, reduction in show costs and increase in morale for this great group of marketers.

Driving Innovation Requires More than a Motivational Poster

There is no silver bullet to creating a culture that embraces innovation and actually succeeds at creating new programs, products and processes that improve performance, profitability and strategy execution. Innovation cannot be mandated or legislated, and it definitely is not inspired by the annual corporate motivational poster. Earlier in my career, working for an electronics manufacturer based in Japan, I recall looking forward (with amused anticipation) to the rollout of the new motivational slogan for the year. The poor translation and short, terse statements emboldening us to "create more faster," and "work towards the 200 year plan," were the source of much amusement and discussion between co-workers based in the U.S. The motivation train officially derailed when the day finally arrived for our general manager to unveil the new poster, and we could hardly contain ourselves when it proudly exclaimed, "Same slogan as last year." The slogan writer must have been in a creative slump, and one can only imagine the decision that the unwitting printer made when faced with some vague instructions. So much for motivation by slogan!

Effective Leadership Practices are the Raw Materials for the Innovation Machine

The practices and approaches that we have emphasized throughout the book are essential to building the innovation machine within your team. Your credibility, your ability to create the effective working environment and the respect that you show your team members by paying attention all serve to create a situation ripe for innovation to flourish. As you move through the early days of a new leadership position, your focus should move from start-up issues like wrapping your arms around strategy, learning about your team members and getting involved with daily business, to issues broader in scope. For example, the year one challenges that a new customer support director faces to staff and train a team, perhaps implement a new software system and get to know the customer's needs, should give way to concerns about how to leverage customer support to differentiate the firm in the marketplace and to the identification and implementation of programs and processes that build value for the firm and send competitors racing to emulate.

The Three Fundamental Conditions for Realizing the Innovation Machine

Building the innovations machine starts with your understanding of and application of the principles in *The Nine Attributes of Great Leaders* and in *The Leader's Charter*. Realizing an innovation-driven team is one of the major destinations on your leadership journey, a trip that begins on day one of your leadership role when you look new team members in the eyes and ask them to trust you. Creating the innovation machine is easiest if you and your team meet the following three conditions:

1.   You as the <u>leader must have high personal credibility</u> in the eyes of your associates. If you lack credibility, no amount of cajoling, cheerleading, imploring or dictating will matter. People do not innovate on command. However, if the team believes in, trusts and is inspired by you as their leader, then the first condition is satisfied. History is filled with great examples where a group struggling to exist has rallied around a credible leader to survive and ultimately prosper.

2.   An <u>effective working environment</u> is essential for a spirit of innovation to take hold and become a part of the culture of a team. The process of innovating requires people to expose radical, sometimes outlandish ideas. People will put themselves at risk only in an environment of high trust. They must be confident that there are no negative repercussions for speaking up, proposing new ways of thinking about problems and solutions or pushing the envelope on "the way its always been done."

3.   The <u>team must have good chemistry and be experienced in creative problem solving</u> as the final condition. Your leadership style and the working environment that you have created are huge determinants of team dynamics—team chemistry, with a few important exceptions. The individuals on your team all bring their personalities, agendas, experiences and biases to the table every-time that they sit down. And while you cannot control those innate individual characteristics, your awareness of the individual styles and approaches is essential to your success in managing the group dynamics and leveraging the team's in-

ternal diversity for the greater good. Additionally, the amount of experience that a particular group has in working together is a factor in problem-solving settings, and either a lot of shared experience or no shared experience working together will impact the interaction and can impact outcomes. Team chemistry is easily observed in brainstorming circumstances, and ultimately, it is your goal to ensure that your team becomes great at this important ideation process.

Good Brainstorming Practices Fuel the Innovation Machine

Nowhere is the chemistry of the team or the effectiveness of the working environment tested more thoroughly than during the brainstorming process. This seemingly simple process of generating ideas is actually quite complex. You need to teach your team to brainstorm effectively by ensuring that the ground rules are clear, that the topic being brainstormed about is understood by all and that roles are assigned for time-keeper, note-taker and facilitator. Your positive support of ideas, questions to clarify and encouragement of "build-on" techniques to take someone's idea and add to it, are important to helping a team learn how to brainstorm effectively. There are many great books and articles on managing effective brainstorming processes, and we encourage you to take advantage of these resources. A few of our favorites are listed in the Resource Center under Leadership at www. management-innovations.com.

We've Built and Fueled the Innovation Machine-
How do we get it started?

In the simplest of words, it takes a common cause—a vexing problem that is viewed by a group as important and worthy of solving. Nothing motivates creativity like a dire problem or a cause that once addressed, promises significant reward to the firm and positive notoriety for the team. Throughout history, many (most) great achievements occurred because groups of people rallied around problems with life or death circumstances. In business, these problems may not be life or death, but they can take on that significance if a group seizes on an issue, problem or opportunity and raises it to near life or death importance. Examples include:

- A smaller firm faces much larger and better-capitalized competitors and to survive, must find a way to compete on a global stage.
- An entrenched firm finds its world turned upside down as a low-cost, lesser featured offering disrupts its comfortable existence.
- Competitors are quick to move to offshore manufacturing and grab a tremendous cost advantage that is impossible to compete against.
- A company finds that industry influencers view a competitor as the market leader, when there is little difference in products or pricing. The competitor's advantage is in more aggressive messaging and promotions.
- A publicly traded firm has good numbers and a great future, but cannot get investors interested in the stock.
- A decade old technology firm still relies on the same sales management and compensation practices that were in place in the early "go go" days, but the world has changed.
- A technology firm in a small community is faced with the challenge to recruit technical talent to fuel product development during a boom time. The remote location of the firm makes this a tough problem.
- The time to close the books takes most of a month for this firm that needs to close within a week to meet new governance requirements.

And we could keep going. The fact is that while none of those problems were literal life or death situations, they were all important to their respective firms and they were ultimately solved by groups of people that had the confidence to experiment, fail and then try again. While many of the examples covered above are reactive, or in response to competitor or market forces, you should seek out opportunities to create common causes that are proactive in nature. During the late 1990's, Jack Welch's "Destroy Your Business.com" initiative challenged his teams to rethink their entire business models with the assumption that the internet would ultimately disrupt these businesses and that it would be better to be out ahead of the challenge instead of reacting to it.

A recent great example of innovation's power to transform companies, industries and even the lives of consumers, comes from Apple's successes with the iPod music player and iTunes music service. The remarkable and pleasing designs of Apple's products, coupled with the lifestyle improving opportunities that they have afforded consumers, have helped to transform three industries: consumer electronics, entertainment and software. Prior to the launch of these now legendary products, Apple was struggling to stay alive in the personal computer business, where companies like Dell, HP and critical suppliers, including Intel and Microsoft were squeezing Apple out of the market. Apple had no chance to beat these entrenched and better capitalized market participants head-on, so they outflanked them by creating revolutionary new offerings and services that were difficult to emulate and left the bigger players scrambling for a response. The iPod and iTunes and the dramatically revamped iMac and notebook computer lines have helped Apple to record revenues and profits while redefining entire markets.

Whether your common cause is survival, revolutionizing a market, transforming a company or outflanking competitors, you need to leverage this cause to start the innovations machine in motion.

Start by Building a Track Record of Innovation Success

Nothing breeds success like success, so it is important for you to help your team get some problem-solving victories under its belt. Whether you are a new leader assigned to head up an existing team or you are assembling a completely new group, you are faced with a number of interesting challenges to jump-start the process. Legacy teams often need to be shaken up a bit to kick-start creativity while new teams need to find a reason to gel together. Your job to kick this process into gear is to find an opportunity for these teams to attack a common cause or vexing problem. These early problem-solving projects provide you with a great opportunity to observe team dynamics, identify potential problems and to establish your expectations for effective problem solving processes and outcomes.

Finding the common-cause or vexing problem and get started

A leader that pursues the start-up lessons and questions in Chapter 5 will not have to look far to find a salient common cause issue or problem that requires teamwork to solve. As you should recall, the question categories ranged from clarifying the mission and role of your team, understanding your firm's strategy and priority objectives and how your team fits into the execution plan, to gaining insights from customer-facing teams and customers on the realities of the marketplace.

A number of follow-on questions to <u>help identify the vexing problems</u> <u>include</u>:

1. Based on your internal and external research what are the most compelling issues that your firm faces to realize its strategy objectives?

2. Can you place the issues on a continuum of "needed for survival" to "nice to get to if we have time?"

3. Are the items closer to "needed for survival" directly linked to revenue growth and profitability?

4. Are the items closer to "needed for survival" impactful to customers and competitors?

5. If solved, do you believe that the issue will significantly impact your organization's performance, market position or service to customers?

While the above questions may seem simple, answering them properly requires a great understand of the market situation and some challenging discussions to distill a lot of ideas and issues down to the real challenges for your team or your firm. If the process is facilitated properly, you will marvel at the evolution of your team as they come to grips with identifying and quantifying the vexing issues, and zero in on a cause of significance to their firm and their careers. You and your team should come out of this process united and excited to conquer new worlds.

Solution Development and the *Innovation Acid Test* Questions

The *Innovations Acid Test* questions are helpful to ensuring that the team thoroughly evaluates the options and drives to the best solutions.

Innovation Acid Test Questions

1. Are we solving the right problem? How do we know?
2. Can the costs and benefits of the solution be quantified?
3. Do we have the skills to implement the solution? If not, can they be easily acquired?
4. Do we understand how the solution impacts other teams in the company? Our customers? Competitors? Partners?
5. Is the solution non-conventional? (This is not always the case, but it helps teams stretch their collective minds.)

6. Is the solution reproducible and sustainable?

7. What are the assumptions underlying our solution, including the time to implement and the time to realize gains?

8. Are we convinced that it is the best possible solution? Why?

9. Are there dissenters? What are their concerns? What would they do?

10. If management says "no" to this approach, what is our second best solution? (This forces the group to stretch intellectually.)

The questions are straightforward, but very difficult to answer properly. The *Acid Test* questions serve as filters on ideas, and challenge you and your team to look at issues and solutions from all perspectives. Teaching your team to evaluate their ideas against these questions will ensure that you are prepared for the grilling that you will likely receive from your management as you roll up your proposal and seek approval. Consider the *Acid Test* questions as career enhancers for you and your team!

Leverage Really Big Challenges to Motivate the Team!

Once the team has developed experience in problem solving, turn up the temperature on the demand for innovation around material topics. The acronym BHAG (big, hairy, audacious goal) was developed to challenge teams to drive dramatic change. In my own experience, teams that have developed a track record of experience for problem solving and innovating are teams that enjoy progressively larger challenges. I have used this approach to great success over time, seizing opportunities to proact and react around major opportunities in pursuit of either restoring a business to leadership or asserting a leadership position for a business in the marketplace. A BHAG initiative is all consuming for a team for a period of time, so use this technique judiciously to improve your business and provide visibility to your team. Remember as well that not everything can be a BHAG. Use them sparingly.

Reinforce Success Through Visibility, Attribution and Reward!

Regardless of BHAG or just an AG (Audacious Goal), you need to reinforce and reward successes with visibility and credit. Your ability to genuinely provide attribution for success is an important part of your role as a leader. Remember as well...YOU are not the subject of any of this success! After the conclusion of a wildly successful program driven by a BHAG to re-invent our entire market communications program, a raucous awards ceremony where involved people from all over the company were given inexpensive thank you gifts, pizza and significant air time (and some good natured ribbing where it had been earned), the group could not wait to go after the next big challenge.

Always reward extraordinary achievements in unique ways

Extraordinary effort and achievement should be singled out and privately acknowledged through appropriate and approved means. Work with your manager or the human resources department to identify financial or non-financial but valuable rewards and thanks for a job well done. I credit my partner in this endeavor, Rich, in educating me about the power of awards other than cash (although cash is not horrible!). Ideas include travel vouchers, gift certificates personalized to a favorite store or to fulfill a new need (i.e. the camera or camcorder for the new parents), hobby items or anything else that you can come up with that shows that you are both thankful for the efforts and results and that you are paying attention to the associate as a person.

Failure is the Best Teacher...Leverage it to Strengthen the Team

You and your team will fail from time to time and that is good. The points in time where failure becomes apparent are great teaching opportunities as well as opportunities for you to strengthen your personal credibility. Many leaders miss this point and seek out opportunities to assign blame, identify scapegoats or cover up the misfire. Instead, you will be best served by taking the failure head-on, admitting the loss and then similar to the brainstorming methodology identified above, leading your team through a "lessons-learned" debrief. What starts out as a quiet and somber session can turn into an energizing and galvanizing event where people stand back and look at what worked, what didn't and how they can improve in the future. More often than not, a properly conducted "lessons-learned" session will send the team storming out the door ready to conquer the next battlefield and avenge the earlier loss. Also, remember to build your personal credibility account by invoking the coach's philosophy, "if we win, it is because of the team and if we lose, it is my fault."

As the Leader, You Need to Know When
You are Helping or Hindering

During the pursuit of a BHAG, you should stay involved to ensure that the team and individuals are on topic, on time and focused. You will realize many opportunities to coach, including dealing with misfires, challenging interpersonal dynamics and all sorts of obstacles that creep up. Your job is never to micromanage the process, but always to stay involved and support, coach, and on rare occasions, intervene.

Over time and as your team gains experience and develops their positive chemistry for innovating and problem-solving, you will need to reassess your role as part of these processes. I have found that with new or problematic teams that my direct involvement as leader was appropriate and effective. Alternatively, with experienced and well functioning teams, it was quite possible for me to hinder the creativity and productivity of the team and that everyone's best interests were served by staying away and waiting to be briefed once the team was ready. Do not assume that because you are the leader, you are required to lead everything. On the contrary, a great measure of your effectiveness is how competent your team is without you sitting at the head of every meeting. Let go and watch your team grow.

Epilogue: How Do You Know When It's Working?

Once you have applied the lessons in this book and have established a team with a track record of success and a few failures, you will face a new set of challenges. Many people wonder how they will know when they have succeeded in building an innovation-focused team, and my answer is from the school of, "you'll know it when you see it." You will observe this team that you inherited or hand-selected begin to become a recognized force for building value and solving problems. The team will gravitate to larger and larger challenges, and your expectations for success even in the face of overwhelming odds will become their own expectations. You will no longer need to be the driver behind the team, but your presence and attention will motivate the group to execute on problem-solving and in what is the topic of the next chapter, your team will begin taking pride in being operationally excellent on a day to day basis. This great team that you have shepherded will likely become more independent from you, with leaders emerging to tackle problems and drive their own innovations, all without you having to raise the issue. It is at this point that you will begin to understand that you have done your job and your pursuit of being a great leader is working.

Over time you will increasingly find yourself as an observer and cheerleader, although your presence as a coach will still prove remarkably valuable, as all great teams experience disruptive events from time to time. Additionally, you are responsible for ensuring that your team's efforts remain intrinsically linked to the organization's strategies and evolving market conditions. Your role as educator will begin to supersede your role as de facto leader. You will also remain involved to manage the natural change that occurs within a team. New hires join the team while experienced veterans are promoted beyond the group. Business conditions change and new problems or challenges arise that might require different skill sets or ways of looking at the world. While your days of teaching the group the ABCs of brainstorming and creative problem solving may be over, your ability to observe and gauge progress or identify problem areas is always in demand. Your ability to recognize problems and to either resolve or cause these problems to be resolved is the value that you bring to a mature and effective team. When you finally reach this point where it seems like you are immaterial to the group doing a great job, you need to remember that this was your destination and this is your silent victory. Silent of course, because "You" are not the subject of your team.

Discussion questions: Teamwork and The Tennis Match

- *Why might one team be better at innovating than another?*
- *The mid-market architecture team was resolute in staying on plan with their new offering, but they ultimately supported the Project "Duct Tape" idea. What does this say about the working environment in mid-market?*
- *What should George do to get his team jump-started?*
- *George is considering keeping both Paul and June out of the next brainstorming session. Do you think he is right about this?*
- *Is it easy for a leader to mandate innovation?*

For ideas on how the authors view the situation at Apex and the issues outlined above, visit the Leadership Resource Center at www.management-innovations. com, and click on Practical Lessons-Discussion Questions.

PREFACE TO CHAPTER 12

PAT'S MODEL BEHAVIOR

Pat sat at her desk looking at the notes from the recent operations brainstorming meeting. There were some good ideas here, and some ideas that might have merit, but that had been assigned a lower priority. Every one of her teams was doing its part to respond to Victoria Pyott's call to action at the Leadership Summit earlier this year. In fact, Pat was proud that her teams had been held up as models for the rest of the organization to follow in pursuit of operational excellence. However, Pat also knew that most of the low-hanging fruit in terms of operational improvements that she could control had been picked, and further improvements were going to involve getting other departments to change their ways. " Easier said than done at Apex," she thought.

Pat had some experience in meeting resistance to change from other parts of the organization. Recently, she had pulled together a group of her peers to discuss possible ideas in the "order to cash" business processes of the company, and for the most part, she was given a chilly reception. At one point, one of her colleagues had chimed in with a sarcastic, "Well since you're the model that Victoria is so pleased with, we'll leave the changing up to you, Pat." It was met with laughter, but nothing much got accomplished during the rest of the meeting.

Pat was convinced that the ideas the team had generated for improving the order to cash" processes would save the firm substantial money and improve customer service at the same time. If only she could get the other groups to join in to pursue this project.

Victoria Measures Apex's Progress

Victoria Pyott was generally encouraged by the progress she was observing at Apex. Since her presentation warning of marketplace threats and leadership malaise at the annual summit a few months ago, she had increased her day-to-day involvement with the teams and their progress was visible. Ideas were being generated and a few strong ones, like "Project Duct Tape" were being implemented. In general, the teams that you expected to support innovation were supporting it, but she was still troubled by the lack of cross-functional collaboration to reduce costs and streamline operations.

"We've not been a measurement focused company," she commented to Paul Burns, Apex's CFO. *"Perhaps the lack of good metrics makes it difficult for people to understand where they are at, what they need to improve, and whether their ideas are working. I'm also concerned about whether people believe that my warnings are real or whether they are dismissing them as CEO rhetoric,"* she added.

CHAPTER 12
IN PURSUIT OF OPERATIONAL EXCELLENCE

Effort is nice, but results count. Regardless of the heady notions of creating an effective work environment or building an innovation machine with your team, one thing is for certain: your company expects you to produce. While it is interesting to think of your role in leadership as some great sociological experiment with you changing the variables and observing the outcomes, chances are your boss does not view it that way. You may enjoy a brief honeymoon period after a promotion to a new role, but don't bank on it. In today's hypercompetitive markets, it is common for the honeymoon to end somewhere between lunch and 3:00 p.m. on your first day. Regardless of whether you've inherited a team that looks like a cross between *The Three Stooges meets Gilligan's Island*, it's your team now, and it's your responsibility to ensure that they are getting the job done to meet or exceed objectives.

If you have ever been a part of an operationally excellent team, you know that the experience is exhilarating. Pardon the sports analogy, but it's like being a member of the best team in the league, and hitting and exceeding your targets is like winning the league championship. You and your teammates walk into work with a swagger knowing that you are part of a special group doing great things for your organization, and that regardless of what the day throws at you, the team out yet another innovative way to win. When you are on a winning team, every member expects to succeed, and this confidence fuels a high-energy environment dedicated to performance. Being a part of a winning team is a great experience, and one that makes working feel a lot less like work.

As a leader, your objective is to realize a winning team where all of your hard work pays off in the form of a group of people dedicated to driving results and committed to success. This state of operational excellence is not the domain of any specific function or group, and whether you are leading a team of finance professionals, a customer support group or a team of sales representatives, it is your goal to field a team that meets and exceeds targets while living up to the core values of the organization.

Effective Leaders Figure Out How to Win by Inspiring Their Teams

Unlike the subdued feedback from our research interviews on how leaders drive innovation with their teams, the topics around setting aggressive goals, hitting and exceeding targets and seeking the next big challenge to overcome, elicited tremendous excitement and some rich ideas from the participants. In particular, the experienced leaders that we interviewed understood their responsibility for results, and were passionate about the importance of winning by inspiration versus domination. When asked about what they do to keep teams focused on driving results, the various leaders suggested the following approaches:

- Leveraging core values and beliefs and establishing and reinforcing priorities for near and longer term.
- Providing team members the space to do what they are good at, and offering support when asked.
- Ensuring that everyone was having fun while working towards difficult goals.
- Supporting team members even in the event of a mistake.
- Linking organizational goals with individual objectives.
- Setting clear expectations for performance and behavior.
- Being realistic about work life balance.
- Managing the work environment—providing feedback and praise, helping to manage stress levels, and facilitating good working relationships between team members.
- Knocking down barriers and providing the team with the resources needed to execute.

IN PURSUIT OF OPERATIONAL EXCELLENCE

These powerful approaches and practices are grounded in many of the lessons covered in this book, including paying attention to the work environment, getting to know your people, learning from mistakes, and leveraging expectation setting as a tool to drive behavior. This last point, setting expectations, is our starting point in pursuit of operational excellence.

Operational Excellence Starts with the Leader
Setting Expectations for Performance

Operational excellence starts with you setting the expectation that your team will perform at a level necessary to achieve or exceed objectives. In seeking to establish standards of performance and behavior, your very public and very frequent statements of expectations are some of the most powerful tools at your disposal. In Chapter 5, we discussed the critical need for you to understand your organization's strategy and to understand how you and your team fit into the picture for delivering on key objectives. Your ability to grasp your true priorities provides the ability for you to articulate these priorities and objectives to your team and begin setting the expectation for success.

When I assume responsibility for a team, from the first moment of my first day and in every meeting, hallway discussion, phone call or e-mail communication thereafter, I reinforce my expectations for behavior, performance and achievement of objectives. You need to do the same. No one should leave a conversation with you without being reminded what their role is in helping the group hit its targets, and importantly, asking their opinion of what needs to be done to get there. Everyone on the operationally excellent team must understand their responsibility for execution around key objectives, and be aware that their performance and progress are both important and are being watched. The operationally excellent team always knows the objectives, where they stand in relation to achieving them, and what they are going to do to get there. Suggestions for establishing your expectations with your new team, include:

- Communicate expectations for achievement of operating objectives from day one of your leadership role. There should be no ambiguity about your intentions and your expectations for performance, progress reporting and ultimately, achievement. Remember to link yourself as ultimately responsible for the outcomes of the team and to let them understand your role to both coach and support the team and individual efforts.

- Kick-off all operations oriented meetings with a review of the key business objectives and progress towards those objectives. Conclude every session with a reminder of the objectives—especially near term deliverables. This is equally important for individual review sessions as it is for group situations.

- Praise, celebrate and reward milestone achievement and positive progress frequently and liberally.

- Acknowledge roadblocks, misfires and general problems quickly and calmly. Your appropriate reaction to these occurrences will contribute to building an effective working environment where people can honestly and openly deal with the negative as well as the positive.

- Leverage the concepts around problem solving and innovation outlined in Chapter 11 to improve collaboration and focus your team on achievement.

- Seek out and deal with poor performers. As the saying goes, one bad apple can ruin the whole bushel, and the same is true with teams. Your handling of poor performers (professionally and timely of course) sends a powerful message to your team. You would much rather have them understand that mistakes are learning experiences, repeated mistakes are a problem and chronic poor performance a reason for reassignment or dismissal, versus having them observe you ignore or not deal with someone who is not pulling their load. The expectation of solid performance is reinforced by your effectively dealing with poor performers. This goes straight to your credibility account.

- Set expectations for your own performance and be open about your progress and your own misfires. The team needs to see that you practice what you preach.

The Three Dimensions of the Operationally Excellent Team

In describing an operationally excellent team, we look at three dimensions: the alignment of the team and individuals around the corporate strategy and key objectives; the fitness for use of the team's output by customer groups, and the timeliness of the output as required by the customer groups and the organization. Let's break down the dimensions a bit further:

1. **Activities must be linked to the firm's strategy and in direct support of achieving key objectives.** Linking to the strategy provides critical context for a team's activities. Individuals on a team must see how their activities connect with the organization's strategy and how their output will be leveraged to achieve key objectives. Often, teams or entire departments become myopic, focusing solely on operating within their own silo and optimizing against their own targets and ignoring broader corporate objectives. This is always a leadership problem, and you need to be sensitive to combating "creeping siloization." The best cure is clear dialogue around the firm's strategy and key targets, and focus on better aligning departmental activities to those objectives.

2. **The output of the team must be in-line with market and customer needs and internal financial targets.** Your customers (internal and external) are the ultimate arbiters of your output, and will vote with their purchase decisions as well as their opinions. Whether your customers are internal to the organization or external in the marketplace, it is incumbent upon you to establish the forums and opportunities to gain their feedback on your products or services (timeliness, quality, appropriateness etc.) and for you to develop the systems needed to turn this feedback into action. If you are a professional services team delivering software integration services to an end-user customer, then quality will be defined by your adherence to your quoted workplan as well as the resultant successful operation of the software following the integration. Alternatively, if you are a marketing communications team focused on providing high quality leads to the sales force, then you will be judged on the pace, quality, frequency and cost of the leads as well as the resultant change in sales pipeline. If you provide order entry services to support your sales team, then your procedures and services must be focused on ensuring high quality, timely entry of orders. Over time, the needs of your customers will change or changes in the marketplace will demand response and innovation. You are still on the hook to innovate with your operationally excellent team, and you are always responsible for ensuring that you stay attuned to changing market dynamics.

3. **Timeliness is essential.** You never want to be identified as leading a team that lacks a sense of urgency or that is satisfied to march at its own pace, with disregard for the pace needed by

other customer or functional groups. The further from the customer that you sit inside an organization, the more likely you or your team are to lack a well developed sense of market timing. If you manage a team that is primarily resident inside an organization, serving internal customers, you will have to fight to ensure that you and your team maintain a keen sense of the pace that these groups require to meet their needs. Remember, the salesperson wants everything done yesterday, and the software developer is quick to say that, "nine women cannot make a baby in a month," and while they are both right, it is your role to enable other groups to succeed in satisfying and capturing customers and supporting strategy execution. Work to develop a solid understanding of the timing needs of your customers and ensure that your team understands the need and adjusts their activities to meet the customer requirements. Don't get caught in the time warp that so frequently traps groups that sit inside of corporations.

Beware of Organizational Myopia—It Kills Careers!

It is common for operationally focused leaders and teams to view the world only from the vantage point of their function at the expense of looking at the bigger picture of their organization. These teams can become and often are operationally excellent within their own boundaries, but their rigidity and near-sighted focus on only their activities, their metrics and their objectives makes them a problem area for the rest of the organization. In my opinion, the leaders of these groups have taken their cause too literally, and have forgotten their responsibility to the overall strategy execution and their obligation to adapt and adjust to changing market characteristics. You will undoubtedly run across the department manager who is reputed to run a great team, and will gladly give you time and even thoughtful consideration of your ideas or requests, but ultimately will shoot down any activities that might change the pursuit of their functional activities. Your ability to work across the organization and positively drive change through consensus building around topics focused on improving or innovating is the primary method to combat operationally myopic leaders. They never respond to brute force or even logic, but they almost always comply with consensus once they realize that they are hopelessly outnumbered. If you find yourself resisting ideas from outside your group due to the impact that they might have on your processes, tasks or measurements, you need to remind yourself that you exist to serve the organization's strategy and not the other way around

Do the Right Things, or Do Things Right?

Earlier in my career, the Vice President that I worked for asked me where I thought we should focus this year. The specific question was, "Should we do the right things, or do things right?" I recall thinking that the question was a bit silly, since the answer was clear, but upon further consideration, I enjoy the philosophical and practical issues that it raises. My answer now is the same as it was then, a resounding "Both!" The "do the right things" component begs prioritization and alignment around the firm's strategy, and as we have discussed at length, that is essential. The "do things right" element begs the execution issue and a commitment to getting things done on time and with the right quality. Focusing on one at the expense of the other seems like a formula for disaster or at least a commitment to sub optimize. I do recall that the VP did not like my answer, as it was clear he was seeking to become operationally focused (at least as he defined it). To him, the "do the right things" vector was the right answer. I still find it odd to consider either one as discrete, and perhaps that is why the concept of operational excellence as we describe it incorporates all three dimensions: alignment with the corporate strategy and key objectives; an understanding of the right priorities; and a commitment to high quality and timely execution. Beware the lure of one or two-dimensional approaches to operational excellence. You need to operate in all three dimensions to do your job effectively.

Tough Love—There are No Trophies for Effort Without Results

I remember rankling at a business and technical writing instructor in college who indicated at the top of the syllabus something to the effect that efforts would not count in her grading, only results. "Of course efforts count," I remember thinking angrily as I realized that this wasn't going to be the easy A that I had been told it would be. After all, my parents, my teachers and my coaches frequently praised my great efforts, even if the results fell a bit short. In fact, I prided myself on trying harder than anyone else, practicing harder, pushing myself to overcome my natural limitations. What heresy was this? A teacher who did not care whether I worked for twenty hours or two on the assignment, but only cared how it came out at the conclusion. She was absolutely right!

You are accountable for your results, and as a leader of a team, you are accountable for their results. Many well-intentioned leaders flounder or worse yet, crash on the rocks of great effort, often because they lost track of their responsibility to drive results. You want to stay off of the "A for Effort but F for Fired" list, and here are twelve key questions to keep you and your team focused on driving performance.

The Top 12 Question Categories to Keep You and Your Team Focused on Driving Results

1. Have I recently refreshed my understanding of the current business strategy, key objectives and overall organizational progress towards key objectives? Have I updated my team on this information?

2. Has anything occurred in the business environment to merit a change in key objectives and what is the impact on the work that my team is doing? Do we need to alter our objectives?

3. Do I regularly receive feedback from customer groups on the quality, timeliness and fitness for use of our products and services? Have I established the processes to review this feedback and adjust activities accordingly?

4. Do I understand my competitors, their strategies and do we have a plan in place to either respond to or outflank these competitors?

5. Have I established performance measures for my team that measure our contribution to key strategy objectives? Have I refreshed the performance measures in concert with strategy refresh activities?

6. Do I regularly update my team on operating results? Have I conducted an operations meeting and review in the last ninety days? If not, when is the earliest that I can schedule one?

7. Am I current on delivering performance reviews and feedback?

8. Do I have the right people in the right positions? Have I held off on some negative personnel changes? Am I late on making some positive personnel adjustments?

9. Am I truly paying attention to my people?

10. How would my associates describe the working environment that we have at the moment? What's working and what's not?

11. What BHAGs are we working on presently? How are we progressing? Are these the right BHAGs?

12. Have I taken the time to acknowledge and reward great performances?

While the list above could go on, these question categories fundamentally address the three dimensions of operational excellence, as well as forcing you to pay attention to the many and important challenges of people and team development that we have emphasized throughout the book. If you find yourself unable to provide good answers to any of the above questions, you are in danger of spinning your wheels and not delivering the results expected of you. Remember, you aren't graded by the quantity of your e-mails or the number of hours you work—your grade as a leader is given for driving the right results at the right time.

Epilogue: In Pursuit of Great Results

There are no shortcuts to building the operationally excellent team. The process starts and ends with you and your commitment to becoming a great leader. Your attention to and application of the concepts outlined in this book will help you tremendously in becoming that great leader and in building teams that drive results, businesses and markets. Like everything else that we have talked about, there are no silver bullets for leadership or for business results, but there are some fundamentals that if applied relentlessly, yield good results. The fundamentals that I describe below are inherent throughout this book and are as much fundamentals for success in life and business as they are "how to" steps for running great operations meetings. It is our opinion that if applied properly, these lessons are about "doing the right things," and "doing things right" that are so essential to your success as a leader.

Epilogue Part II—In Pursuit of Effective Leadership

Doing the right things right—creating a culture of success

1. <u>People will do great things for the right leaders</u>. Frequently review the "nine attributes of great leaders," from Chapter 1 and seek opportunities to strengthen your credibility as a leader. Your attitude counts; you are always on and your actions must support your words.

2. <u>Always understand your mission</u> and translate this mission into your team's priorities. Be aware that missions and priorities change and you need to monitor your customers and markets

and be mature enough to recognize and embrace change when it is necessary.

3. <u>You are as effective as your able to effectively communicate</u>. Great leaders are great communicators, and great teams always know the game they are playing, the results needed to win and where they are on the game clock. Your job is to constantly provide context for your team.

4. <u>An effective working environment is fundamental</u> to everything that you do. Your job is to live up to *The Leader's Charter*:

> *Your primary role as a leader is to <u>create an environment</u> that facilitates high individual and team performance against company and industry standards, supports innovation in processes, programs and approaches, encourages collaboration where necessary for objective achievement and promotes the development of your associates in roles that leverage their talents and interests and that challenge them to new and greater accomplishments.*

5. <u>Your currency is respect</u>. You respect people by treating them honestly and by paying attention to their work, their development and their lives. People that feel respected are remarkably productive for and loyal to their leaders.

6. <u>Positive expectations consistently reinforced are powerful contributors to success</u>. Your team needs to understand the expectations that you have for performance, behavior and participation and ultimately, they will begin to adopt and internalize your expectations for excellence.

And finally, never forget that life is a journey and the joy is in the trip, not in reaching the destination. Have fun building your teams, building new friendships and take joy in the victories and solace together in the setbacks. Never quit learning, not for a second and never ever give up.

Discussion questions: Pat's Model Behavior and Victoria Measures Apex's Progress

- *How should Pat try and break down the functional barriers that she is running into in her quest to improve "order to cash?"*
- *Should Pat enlist Victoria's help?*

- *How important is it to have shared and visible metrics when driving change initiatives?*
- *Why would people resist ideas to improve operational efficiency?*
- *What should Victoria do to convince people that her warnings are not CEO rhetoric?*

For ideas on how the authors view the situation at Apex and the issues outlined above, visit the Leadership Resource Center at www.management-innovations. com, and click on Practical Lessons-Discussion Questions.

AFTERWORD
LOOKING AHEAD IN YOUR CAREER

A few of my favorite lines in all of literature include:

"You'll be on your way up!

You'll be seeing great sights!

You'll join the high fliers who soar to high heights:

And:

"You can get all hung up in a pricklely perch.

And your gang will fly on. You'll be left in a Lurch."

Many of you will recognize the sound of Dr. Seuss in those whimsical rhymes, and a few of you will correctly place the source as his classic, <u>Oh, the Places You'll Go!</u> I think of this book and its message of excitement, hope, challenge and perseverance every time I promote someone into their first leadership role. There are no words to adequately and accurately describe the journey that one will experience when they choose the path of leadership. At the time of your initial assignment, you cannot imagine the joy and sense of accomplishment as well as the pain and frustration that you will experience during this journey. Earlier, Rich compared the experience of developing others to the task of parenting, and that is perhaps the best comparison available. You will feel a sense of pride as you watch people that you invested a part of yourself in soar to great heights, and you will feel a profound sense of failure when others with equal investment flounder, or worse, rebel. When you've done everything right and your team and business are flying high, you will marvel at what you've created. And when in spite of your best efforts, things go against you, you will feel a burning frustration and profound loneliness as you ponder what you could have done better or differently. While these words are easy to write from the view back over twenty years of leading, I can imagine that you are more concerned about getting on with your adventure than in understanding mine and ours, so the rest of this section will offer parting advice to help you along the way.

The most valuable tools at your disposal on this odyssey are your gray matter and what's in your heart. The leadership journey is a marathon and from time to time, you will need to refuel, refresh and dig deep inside yourself to find strength for the next leg. As we've highlighted, you alone are responsible for your career and the same holds true for your professional development. While you should aspire to be the type of leader that actively supports and encourages the development of people around you, it is possible and likely that you will not always benefit from working for an enlightened manager. It is most important during those times that you remember to take care of yourself, to find ways to refuel and to keep the leadership fire burning in your gut. Everyone finds inspiration, motivation and renewal in different ways, and you will need to find yours. Also, you will learn as you progress through different phases (age, rank in the organization, size of team etc.), that your needs for education, insight and inspiration change. Be sensitive to where you are and what your needs are to help you through the current phase as well as to prepare for what you might want to tackle in the next stage of your career. Here in no particular order, are some suggestions to help inspire, prepare and recharge you for what lies ahead on this journey of self-discovery.

- Develop your skills as an observer. Most people do not truly pay attention to what is going on around them. You should make an extraordinary effort to pay attention to people, to events and to the interplay of individuals in constant motion around you. Pay close attention to the words, body language and style of leaders that you respect. Do the same to those that you do not respect. Listen hard to what people say and listen harder to what they really mean. Learning by observation is powerful, and I am convinced that there is something to learn, good or bad, from everyone that you come in contact with. Remember the 2:1 ratio (ears to mouth) and apply it liberally.

- Keep a journal of best and worst leadership practices, and add to it every time you observe something that someone or some team does that generates extraordinary or miserable results. Be certain to include your own experiments and experiences. Reference this journal when preparing for a new position, a new challenge, or dealing with a difficult situation.

- Recharge and learn for at least thirty minutes everyday. You should seek out content related to your discipline as well as to leadership and management. Keep a list of good ideas that you garner from this reading and put them into play at the next opportunity. If you don't have time to read, download podcasts or subscribe to audio content and listen during your commute or over your lunch.

- Encourage your team to read or immerse themselves in content related to their discipline for thirty minutes everyday. Provide suggested reading lists, and provide opportunities in meetings to discuss reactions to the various books or articles.

- If you find yourself growing a bit bored and restless with your current position, consider changing positions within your company, even if the move is a lateral one. The challenges of a new assignment are stimulating, and if you like your company and industry, it is preferable to move within than to seek out a competitor.

- Never go to work for a competitor—unless you like degrading your investment in time and energy with your present employer. The grass is NEVER greener at a competitor. If you need to change jobs, consider moving to a non-competitive firm in the industry (a supplier) or consider an entire industry change.

- Consider changing industries to recharge your batteries. If you find yourself growing weary of the same old routine, the same faces at tradeshows and the same now dull industry, make a change. The process of learning a new industry's dynamics, competitors, influencers and market forces is exciting and intellectually stimulating. You will find that business and the challenges of leadership are identical from industry to industry…but the people, products and nuances change just enough to provide a compelling learning experience.

- Once you hit the ten-year mark in leading teams and people, take an assignment as a soloist to test your commitment to a leadership career. A stint in a staff role can be liberating and refreshing. You re-learn how to work and your only performance headaches can be resolved by looking in the mirror.

- Finish your undergraduate degree, and/or start and finish a graduate degree. An MBA is a ticket to admission to credibility for some firms and managers, and a clear sign that you had the interest in your own development to invest the time and energy in completing the degree. If the MBA does not interest you, pursue a Master's program in something related to what you do (Computer Science, Communications etc.). It really doesn't matter what you choose as long as you are interested in the topic matter. At the end, you will have enjoyed a great learning experience and will be able to show the rest of the world that you had the drive and intestinal fortitude to start and finish this assignment.

- If your graduate degree is ten years old or older, you need to refresh the degree. Pursue continuing education or if appropriate, executive education at the graduate business school in your area. After ten years, the content you covered in graduate school is generally obsolete. In addition to gaining new knowledge, you will have the opportunity through one of these programs to meet and work with a whole new network of professionals that share a common desire to improve themselves.

- Read outside of your field. Read biographies, read about history, about the rise and fall of cultures, and read about what makes the world and the universe tick. Exposure to this content provides broad context for your role in the scheme of things, and insights into how to effectively inspire and motivate people.

- Become an industry expert. Seriously! Seek out opportunities to speak or write for audiences and publications in your industry. Do it once it is a great experience. Do it a few times and people start referencing you as an expert.

- Volunteer in your community, with your church or your charity of choice. The rewards are self-evident.

AFTERWORD

And finally, remember to conduct yourself with dignity, integrity and honesty at every step along the way. You will leave a mark on everyone that you lead and many that just observe how you lead. Make certain that the mark is positive, impactful and life enhancing for those that you touch. You will only pass this way once, so do it right.

-Art and Rich

ISBN 142512249-3